TVGoHome

www.tvgohome.com

ff

faber and faber

TVGoHome

Website created by
CHARLIE BROOKER

Written by
CHARLIE BROOKER
with
BEN CAUDELL, PETER HOLMES, NEIL WEBSTER, JONATHAN 'LOG' BLYTH and SIMON SWATMAN

Additional material by
DAMON GREEN, MARK GRIFFITHS, GRAHAM LINEHAN and SID PEACH

Design by
M2 GRAPHIC DESIGN

Despot photograph by
OLLY WIGGINS

Co-ordinators des images:
SIMON SWATMAN and OLLY HERMON-TAYLOR

Additional design by
CHARLIE BROOKER and SIMON SWATMAN

Picture bending:
SCOTT ROBINSON

Illustrations:
KELLY BURLACE, MILO WATERFIELD, JENNY KLAUS SIMON SWATMAN and CHARLIE BROOKER

Ubiquitous photo goon:
NICK SESSIONS

Need to know:
DAVE GREEN and DAN O'BRIEN

Tronpipe floatation assistance:
PHIL WAND

Burly oil rig security:
PAUL GILHEANY

Photos by **REX FEATURES / CORBIS**

The images on pages 108-109 are reproduced courtesy of www.E4.com (where they can also be viewed) and are the copyright of 4 Ventures Limited.

Front cover lounge courtesy of Mr and Mrs Monster.

Special thanks to: Katie Pierce, All at M2 Design: Philippa Baile, Jesse Simon, Tony Lyons, Duncan Youel, David Edgell, Nicola Hammond, Kate Stretton, David Miller, Andy Miller, Kate Balmforth, Rachel Connelly, Clive Priddle, Mitzi Angel, Rosalind Kerr, Steph Keelan & Olly Wiggins, Richard Warburton, Bridget Polley, Sasha Nixon, Mara Goes, Debra Evans, Rob Moore, Stuart Heritage, Tamsin Hughes, Nick Clarke, Vanessa Wong, Linus Wong, Steve Berry, David McCandless, and everyone who ever contributed or so much as clicked their mouse upon the accursed thing.

First published in Great Britain in 2001 by
Fourth Estate
A Division of HarperCollinsPublishers
77–85 Fulham Palace Road
London W6 8JB
www.4thestate.co.uk

This edition published in 2010 by Faber and Faber Ltd
Bloomsbury House
74–77 Great Russell Street
London WC1B 3DA

Copyright © Charlie Brooker, 2001
Introduction to 2010 edition © Charlie Brooker, 2010

1 3 5 7 9 10 8 6 4 2

The right of Charlie Brooker to be identified as the author of this work has been asserted in accordance with Section 77 the Copyright, Designs and Patents Act 1988.

A catalogue record for this book is available from the British Library.

ISBN 978-0-571-27219-8

A CIP record for this book is available from the British Library.

This book is a work of fiction. The names, characters and incidents portrayed in it are the product of the author's imagination. Although some references to actual persons have been included, such persons appear in fictionalised incidents in the book and any resemblance to actual persons, living or dead, events or localities is entirely coincidental.

Printed in Great Britain by Butler Tanner and Dennis Ltd

CONTENTS

FEATURES

5 **101 AMAZING TELEVISION FACTS**
6 **BEFORE THE BOX**
The incredible history of popular entertainment through the ages before the advent of the screen we know and love.
10 **THE GREATEST TV DETECTIVES OF ALL TIME**
A look back at the most memorable wrongbusters ever to grace our screens.
21 **FUNHOLE / MUTTWORLD**
28 **DAILY MAIL ISLANDER**
A special souvenir issue of the newspaper written and run by the citizens of Daily Mail Island.
39 **LIFESOLVER**
Everyday problems troubleshot into submission by our experts.
46 **HOW WE USED TO WATCH**
TV Schedules from the TV Go Home archives.
54 **FUNHOLE / MUTTWORLD**
55 **SCORCH MAGAZINE**
Your free copy of the popular celebrity magazine.
74 **HOW WE USED TO WATCH**
TV Schedules from the TV Go Home archives.
75 **101 AMAZING TELEVISION FACTS**
83 **NOWBITER**
The cutting-edge lifestyle guide edited by Nathan Barley.
100 **CLASSIFIED ADS**
Summer Holidays and Home and Garden.
102 **TV OF TOMORROW**
A look at the television of the future.
104 **SHITTIQUETTE**
An expert guide to vacating your bowels in unfamiliar surroundings.
110 **101 AMAZING TELEVISION FACTS**

LISTINGS

14 **SATURDAY**
22 **SUNDAY**
40 **MONDAY**
48 **TUESDAY**
68 **WEDNESDAY**
76 **THURSDAY**
94 **FRIDAY**

zeppotron.com ff *faber and faber*

83

CUNT

Chaz Panther's **shocking** new video!

This week's most needless celebrity piddlepuff
£1.35

scorch

INSIDE: WHY
THE STARS
ARE SO FAB

55

INCREDIBLE **MARK
JEFFRIES'
CRATE SNUB**

MINNIE DRIVER &
TED BELLINGHAM:
IT'S LOVE!

EXCLUSIVE!
**Robbie Williams
hogs front cover!**
For sixth week running

4

104

RALPH FIENNES

When they say 'shit happens'...
they don't know the half of it

NOTICE
BUMPOO DISEASE
PLEASE KEEP OUT
ANIMALS ON THESE PREMISES
ARE UNDER OBSERVATION

Widdleplop Farm

15

ASS ERUPTERER MOVIES present a JENKY SHITBLAST production of a LEMONADE YAMAHA film RALPH FIENNES "WIDDLEPLOP FARM" HELEN MIRREN JAMIE BELL
Special Appearance by TED BELLINGHAM Screenplay by CLEMENT GANGERAMP Read the Havana Paperback which thankfully doesn't use the ABSURDLY NARROW FONT which is
FORCING YOU to SQUINT at the PAGE RIGHT NOW. Much more of THIS and YOU'LL have a HEADACHE SO BAD your skull MIGHT IMPLODE, eh? Cuh. YEAH.

101
Amazing television facts

1. Studies have shown that if you sit two complete strangers in a bare room, television is one of the three most likely topics of conversation. The other two are the weather and tennis.

2. **Recent archaeological digs have unearthed evidence of a primitive Inca television set. Unlike modern units it had no screen, and resembled a decorative cup. Instead of broadcasting programmes, historians believe it was mainly used for drinking liquid.**

3. If all the houses in Luton were to hit the 'mute' button on their TV remotes at exactly the same time, the silence would be similar to that experienced by the soul after a hanging.

4. **The radiation that comes from the back of a modern television contains enough energy to catapult an egg over a fence.**

5. Donny Osmond is currently appearing on 4 channels. They are The Flimsy Jowel Network (France), Palmcheek Slap Channel (Spain), Housey Housey Bonbon (Greece), and Donny's own channel, The Enormous Osmond Offensive (US).

6. **TVs in the wild can be teased out of hiding with electric cheese on the end of a bent coat hanger.**

7. If you open the back of a television, it is full of drunk women swimming around in brandy.

8. **The same refraction of light that produces a rainbow can be used to recreate TV in puddles. All you need is a sheet of card with a red, green and blue hole in it, and a black torch.**

9. In Wyoming, 1985, a young farmer married his TV, claiming that 'it had cracking tits and fucked like a whore in a coffin'. Both claims later turned out to be delusions – the same delusions that led him to believe that his chimney was menstruating.

10. **The inventor of the television, John Logie Baird, had a beard that resembled an upside-down wedding cake. He hid it by talking into a bucket.**

11. Two offshoot inventions based on TV technology include Mystery Cabinets and Cathode Ray Killguns.

12. **Today's remote controls started life as a simple whip. Early telly addicts could whip a fly from a teacup in the next room.**

13. When no humans are watching TV, pets left at home during the day prevent it from becoming a philosophical problem.

14. **To paint as fast as a TV displays images would require 50,000 Pollocks, but they would probably get in each others' way.**

15. Bang & Olufsen have designed a TV that follows you around the house, using a camera and knowledge of phrenology to assess your preference of channels. A TV that chases a tennis ball and becomes upset when you don't treat it right should be with us by 2011.

16. **Leicester-based food company ScreenSnax has developed a range of crisps that taste like popular TV programmes. Their biggest seller is based on _Crimewatch UK_.**

17. _Chorlton and the Wheelies_ was a documentary.

18. **By the time they reach the age of 36, the average British male will have watched 900 scenes on TV where a doctor pokes his head round a surgery door and calls 'next!'**

19. The most expensive television special ever made was Cyber-Liberace's _Diamond Dance Marathon_, in which a platinum android with the cryogenically-frozen head of Liberace danced on top of the world's largest diamond inside a gigantic snowshaker filled with liquid gold, rubies and rare stamps. It was a ratings flop.

20. **The earliest newsreaders read reports through a sieve.**

21. During the war, television signals were transmitted underground to prevent them getting picked up by the Nazis. Broadcasts could only be seen by peering through a hosepipe at a TV down a well.

Before the BOX

Without entertainment, where would we be? Staring at the walls until our jowls shake with boredom, probably. As long as tedium exists, mankind will always require distraction from it in some form or another – perchance a song, a poem, an exciting detective novel, or a man in a glittery suit telling an off-colour joke about three nuns in a skin hammock.

The most popular form of entertainment the world has ever seen is, of course, television; but how did we cope before it was invented – and how has the so-called "idiot-box" developed since its birth? Join us now as we trace the incredible history of popular entertainment through the ages before the advent of the screen we know and love.

THE PREHISTORIC ERA

The most important thing to realise about prehistoric entertainment is that *The Flintstones* was an absolute tissue of lies. Neanderthal man did not travel to drive-in cinemas in cars that used his own legs as a means of propulsion; nor did he go bowling with the cheerful dot-eyed caveman next door. Instead, when not wrestling bears or standing atop knolls waving their fists at volcanos, our most ancient ancestors kept themselves entertained by repeatedly bashing themselves on the back of the mind with a rock until pictures and sounds appeared in their heads.

Skull-knocking had its advantages – it was cheap and exciting, and anyone cracking themselves in just the correct spot could enjoy a three-hour abstract movie starring an attractive cast of pulsing shapes and twinkling stars. But there were also serious drawbacks, most grave of which was the obvious danger of massive cranial damage: approximately 30% of viewers wound up as mute vegetables, rocking back and forth in a shadowy corner of the den, dribbling cave-juice down their fat furry chins. Historians estimate such widespread idiocy held back mankind's technological progress by six thousand years.

Ugh um painting

Fortunes changed abruptly following the invention of cave-paintings: here was a medium all could enjoy, without risk of cranial injury. Cave-paintings weren't perfect – most people could paint a more convincing likeness of a sabre-toothed tiger with a brush sticking out of their arse – but they were the first form of entertainment that could be watched by the entire community at once. Culture was born – and cultural snobbery soon followed, with the Neanderthal intelligentsia shunning populist action thrillers (such as *Gazelle Hunt* and *Man Throw Spear at Mammoth*) in favour of highbrow erotica (*Woman Pass Spirit Through Hole*) and ambitious surrealism (*Clay and Hair: an Essay in Texture*).

Ultimately, cave-painting died along with the cave-dwellers themselves, who were phased out in favour of proper people at some point before the birth of Christ.

Speak Caveman

Cavemen also kept themselves occupied with rudimentary conversation. Here's a brief guide to some of the most frequently-used caveman phrases.

Ungh mungh mungh mnnnf-unnngh
Pass us that rock, will you?

Gurf ungh mungh-marrf
Don't know about you, but all these dinosaur skeletons are giving me the creeps.

Mngh ungh mungh-mnnnf munnngh gurff
God, I'm bored. It's shit being a caveman.

ANCIENT GREECE

The civilised ancient Greeks may have originated theatre as we know it, but the medium struggled until the invention of Keith Barron in 1936. Greek plays fell into one of two camps: tragedies, in which the protagonist endured catastrophic misfortune, and comedies, in which a man sporting a gigantic prosthetic phallus tumbled about on stage. Comedies proved more popular.

Performers took to the stage with their faces obscured by wooden masks carved into a single evocative expression – a technique routinely used today by doctors who have to break bad news and are anxious not to ruin the moment by inadvertently smirking in the middle of the word "terminal".

A question of sport

The Greeks also invented the Olympic games – identical to a modern sporting event except for three main differences. First, the first athletes had to contend with less lucrative corporate endorsement deals – champion hurdler Perestopholes, for instance, was sponsored by hay. Secondly, in the absence of slow-motion action replays, the most stunning victories had to be re-enacted by lookalike stand-ins, weighted down with lead to ensure they would move at a massively reduced speed. Finally, and most notoriously, all contestants performed naked; a practice that continued for centuries, until the mid-1980s when officials took one look at Zola Budd and abruptly abandoned the policy forever.

LEGACY of the GREEKS

The Greeks also amused themselves by inventing geometry (the study of triangles), philosophy (thinking aloud about triangles until everybody else gets bored and goes home), and democracy (taking a vote on which bit of the triangle to think about next). But impressive though they undoubtedly are, these innovations are ultimately overshadowed by the ancient Greeks' finest contribution to popular culture – those funny urns covered in scenes of exaggerated buggery. They're a *riot*. You get to see it going in and everything.

ANCIENT ROME

The Romans had two obsessions – sex and death – and they indulged them to the full.

Death

The Romans' gory gladiatorial spectaculars were notorious scab-caked cavalcades of sword-slash gash-gaze clap clap fun. Visitors to the Colosseum were assailed by all manner of gruesome sights, from a fallen combatant getting his head sliced off with an axe, to a fat man's bell end poking out the side of his toga as he bent down to take his seat in the amphitheatre.

The more grisly the action in the killing grounds became, the louder the crowd yelled its approval; the sight of a single Christian's lung being chewed out by a lion could generate more noise than a squadron of Cybermen banging trays against their heads. Eventually the Romans' appetite for violence backfired on them: deafened by their own bloodthirsty roaring, they were taken by surprise when a horde of barbarians wearing cotton wool boots snuck up from behind to beat them all to death with cudgels.

Sex

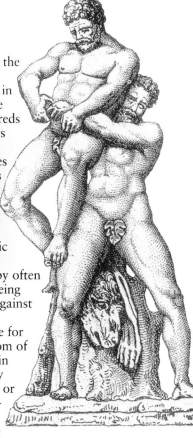

Roman orgies were the stuff of legend: marathon exercises in sexual extravagance during which hundreds of game participants would slowly coagulate themselves into a heaving mass of shuddering buttocks and oily flanks, grinding and pumping away like a single, gigantic undulating flesh Viennetta. Passers-by often found themselves being literally sucked in against their will.

People could survive for decades at the bottom of the fuck-heap, within which it was usually possible to find one or more spacious cave-like clearings with walls formed by the flanks of copulating participants held together by a mature cement of accumulated body fluids. Once safely ensconced within such a den, entire generations could be born and raised without ever seeing daylight, subsisting entirely on the continuous stream of human sap that bubbled down each fleshy wall of their womblike home.

Eventually, these cave-dwellers evolved to suit their surroundings – developing hairless bodies, bulbous rodent-like eyes that could see in semi-darkness, and lengthy snouts capable of seeking out and slurping up entire rivers of semen.

But their lives were fraught with danger. As the juddering fuck-hill they lived inside gradually increased in size over time, the trickle of juices would steadily increase – eventually filling their caves to the brim, drowning all the occupants. During such a flood, the cavepeople would be forced to eat their way out, munching through the fornicating throng with their razor sharp teeth to eventually emerge, blinking, into the daylight, only to be set upon by a horrified mob sporting erections.

MEDIEVAL EUROPE

They were short of many things during the Dark Ages – except corpses. The bubonic plague left graveyards overflowing, and bodies piled up in the streets like fat, rotting leaves. Surrounded on all sides by decaying family members whose swollen tongues dangled grotesquely from their mouldering faces, the survivors were in need of a little light escapism. Fortunately a new artform providing precisely that had just been invented: puppetry.

Early puppet shows were primitive affairs. Objects were sometimes employed instead of characters; the puppeteer would simply hold up a block of wood or a lump of rock, and bob it backwards and forwards as if it were "walking". Compared to the spectacular visuals of a modern Hollywood picture such as *Con Air II*, these special effects are laughable – but at the time they were cutting-edge and audiences would sit entranced for hours.

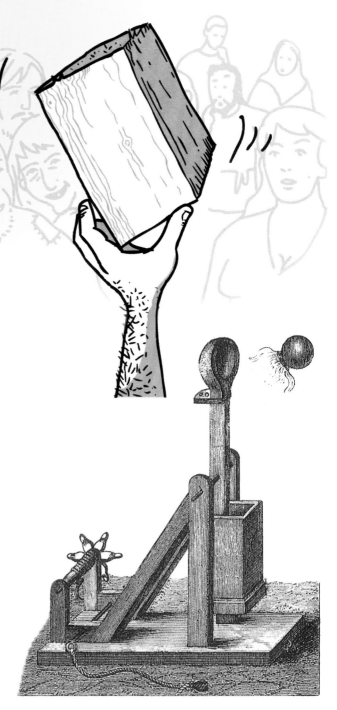

Execution!

Another popular form of medieval mass entertainment was the public execution of criminals; peasants would queue up to watch sadistic and complicated ceremonies that would often last for days.

First the criminal would be stripped of his prison rags and beaten with a broom for hours before having his hands sawn off and cast into a fire. He would then be given the chance to win his own freedom if he could successfully move the crowd to tears by playing a lute using only his stumps: no one ever succeeded, and the futile attempts they did make were generally met with hostility and derision – although the tune 'Chopsticks' was composed by a desperate victim during one such execution.

The greatest
TV detectives
of all time

Crime. A word that strikes fear into all right-thinking people, especially when accompanied by a sudden orchestral stab. **Crime**. The cancer that chews at our social order like a mangy old dog with a rag in its mouth. **Crime**. The ageing war veteran mugged by his next-door neighbour. The simple boy poked and goaded by men dressed as bears. The young girl killed in a hedgerow. All crime is bad. So it's little wonder that if there's a single TV 'type' who's never gone out of fashion, it's the crime-fighting detective. Here we take a look back at the most memorable wrongbusters ever to grace our screens…

Jellyback (1995)

In 1995 Robson Green took on the role of Adam "Jellyback" McKinnon – the floppy police inspector born without a spine. Since he was incapable of standing up, Jellyback was forced to adopt an unusual style of walking, which involved lying prostrate and dragging himself forward with his feet – a time-consuming process that also caused him to bash his head painfully against the tarmac each time he stepped off a kerb. In one memorable episode Jellyback knocked himself unconscious six times while chasing an escaped convict down a lengthy marble staircase.

But his horizontal nature had its advantages. Whenever a ground-level felony took place, Jellyback was first on the scene: whether he was tracking down an escaped snake at a skirting board convention, or solving a murder at a dwarves-only limbo-dancing contest, he was the undisputed expert in floor-level crime.

Green prepared for the role by lying down for two months and imagining he was a strip of bacon; when filming finished and he eventually stood up again he began suffering from vertigo, and would often be sick with nerves, all over his shoes, and the carpet, and in one instance, straight into a goldfish pond in Jerome Flynn's back garden. Jellyback eventually hung up his hat in 1997. It took him six tosses to get it on the hook.

Slamback and Pokehole (1985)

The mid-eighties success of *Miami Vice* led to a wave of imitators, the most unconventional being *Slamback and Pokehole*, a darkly amusing claymation series revolving around the exploits of two ultra-fashionable animated gorillas who cruised the streets of Chicago solving mysteries and tracking down criminals.

As if a duo of primates wasn't novel enough, the series had another unique twist: rather than arrest their quarry, Slamback and Pokehole preferred to dole out their own form of instant justice – rough, protracted anal sex, performed one at a time to the sound of contemporary rock.

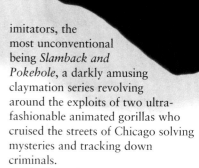

But the public weren't quite ready to watch a pair of unreal plasticine gorillas relentlessly

postman shit prompted a record wave of protests and a spate of revenge bombings. As a result, claymation was outlawed for seven years, and President Bush went on live TV to drown *Slamback and Pokehole*'s creators in a gigantic bucket in front of a jeering mob.

Spoonfed P.I (1991)

Spoonfed P.I. was not like other cops. He was a bland idiot with an M-reg Mondeo and a map of the Lake District in his glovebox. But for one hour every Sunday in 1991 we loved him.

Right from the opening title sequence it was obvious this was a cop show with a difference: Ian Spoonfed reversing out of the car park of the Keswick railway museum just in time to see an elderly hiker beat his wife to death with an anchor, in full view of a coachload of tourists armed with cameras. The theme song only confirmed our suspicions: 'Crimes happen right under his nose / he solves them without much fuss.' The logic behind Spoonfed was straightforward – viewers like countryside more than police

procedure, so with everything straightened out in under ten minutes, they were free to simply sit back and marvel at the rolling hills of the Lake District, as Spoonfed pottered around posting letters, fixing his barn, and taking his daughter on picturesque drives.

The show eventually sold to the States, where bosses at Transversal TV replaced Spoonfed's daughter with a gigantic machine gun, and moved the location from the tranquil Cumbrian countryside to the inside of a zero-gravity tit factory.

Garcia (1968)

During the sixties, kids may have worn flowers in their hair, but that didn't stop them being robbed, mutilated and murdered. It was a special time requiring a special kind of law enforcement – a time to turn on and tune in for drop out hippy detective Jim Garcia.

sodomizing petty criminals, and as complaints poured in, the show's creators went on the defensive, attempting to inject some light humour into the continual buggery scenes by introducing a comic Chihuahua called Mugsy, who stood on the sidelines playing the fiddle, making sarcastic comments, and occasionally leaping in to slurp puddles of spunk through a straw. These changes failed to reverse a ratings nosedive and the series was cancelled in 1986.

Mugsy eventually resurfaced in a series of humorous commercials for the US postal service – a venture that also ended in disaster when a billboard showing him enthusiastically eating a bowl of

Played by ex-Diamond Wolfbox bass player Jefferson Love, Garcia solved crimes with the aid of psychedelic drug, LSD. What the show lacked in plot and coherent dialogue, it more than made up for with impenetrable kaleidoscope mosaics and unlistenable atonal soundscapes.

Fans of the handle-barred hero agree that series one contains all the classic episodes: Bummer at Haight-Ashbury, The Chillum Murders, and most popular of all, the feature-length Belt Buckle Four Hour Stare Mystery. The second, more experimental series made little sense; often Garcia failed to appear on-screen at all, and the bulk of each episode would be taken up with an echoing guitar chord and slow-motion footage of a naked woman tossing her hair around. The show came to an abrupt end during the third season, when Love, a regular user of hallucinogens himself, attempted to perform a citizen's arrest on a San Francisco tram and lost both legs. His subsequent attempt to reinvent himself in the early 70s as a Lovin' Spoonful style Ironside was misjudged – times had moved on. Love now lives as a recluse in San Diego, eking out a living melting eagles in his head.

The Saxon Mysteries (1977)

The Saxon Mysteries followed the work of four-year-old private investigator Jeremy Saxon. Played with verve and gusto by a young Johnny Lee Miller (actually only 3 when filming began), Saxon's naïve and bewildered approach to crime-fighting gripped the nation, with his catchphrase – 'Jeremy done a wee-poo' – being uttered up and down the country. By pricks.

Saxon met a premature end with 'The Case Of The Hidden Banana', an episode in which he finds himself on the trail of a pink banana which next-door neighbour Mr Fleming appears to have lost in mummy's hairy lap-mouth. The denouement, in which Saxon frees the banana and is encouraged by Mr Fleming to peel it, chew it and suck out the juices, led to questions in Parliament and the immediate cancellation of absolutely everything in Britain.

Scott Pocker, CEO (2002)

Sometimes it takes the sheer determination of one man to make a new detective reach our screens. 'I'd been playing around with the format for *Scott Pocker CEO* for years,' says 38-year-old Scott Pocker CEO. 'The idea was that he would be a detective who was also the high-flying, multi-billionaire CEO of a global multimedia entertainment group. You know – just an ordinary guy.'

But the networks proved blind to the brilliance of his vision, and it wasn't until Pocker himself used the millions he made speculating on new technology companies to buy a studio and TV station that Scott Pocker CEO began to take shape.

'At first I thought maybe Ted Danson or Tom Selleck would be perfect as Pocker,' says Pocker. 'But then I got to thinking, maybe someone with more experience as a high-flying CEO of an entertainment group would bring more depth and truth to the role.' Despite casting himself in the lead role, writing the scripts, directing the 90 minute pilot episode and forcing local stations to broadcast it by withholding rights to sports fixtures franchised by the Pocker Entertainment Group, Scott Pocker CEO denies Scott Pocker CEO is a vanity project.

'No way,' says Pocker, 'I only wrote the scripts because the ones that Chris [Carter, *X-Files* creator] did lacked any insight into the world of a good CEO. They were way too dark and brooding. The Pocker in them was obsessed with the nature of consumerism and greed, when he should have been driving round in cars, dining with beautiful women and solving crimes. And the scripts I got from Mamet were even worse.' Despite major networks refusing to carry the show, Pocker is committed to bank-rolling another 26 part series. 'I know people will love Scott Pocker CEO,' says Scott Pocker CEO. 'It's about time people were allowed to see what a great life I have – I mean, he has.'

McAllister's Screamboat (1981)

You can tell a lot about a lawman from the vehicle he keeps. Stringfellow Hawke had Airwolf;

Michael Knight flirted with Kit; and for one balmy summer in 1981, Ray McAllister seemed to be perpetually at the helm of the Screamboat: a river police patrol vehicle powered solely by continual high-pitched shrieking from its 17 occupants.

As eighties cop shows go, *McAllister's Screamboat* was shit. Lee Majors never looked comfortable as Ray McAllister, the half-Cherokee river patrolman, and the relentless screeching necessary to power his craft up and down the dirty brown river made for unbearably irritating viewing. River crimes are also notoriously dull. After the inevitable smuggler capers of the first two episodes, McAllister was soon left kicking his heels, screaming ten yards here to return a stray Frisbee, ten yards there to remove a condom from a swan's beak.

The show was dramatically pulled in Britain after a maniac went on the rampage in a Wakefield school. On hearing terrified screams from the playground, teachers assumed the children were aping the teatime show. They weren't. They were being attacked by a shirtless man holding a claw hammer.

Bathysphere P.I. (1988)

Seamlessly blending together two of televisions most popular formats: crime and underwater drama, late 80s cop show *Bathysphere P.I.* proved the ideal vehicle for Judge Reinhold, after his earlier disastrous outing in the ill fated *Judge's House!* – a sitcom in which Reinhold played landlord to an apartment block full of alcoholic Supreme Court judges.

Reinhold starred as Nick Falcon, a disillusioned homicide detective who solves crimes at the bottom of the Atlantic Ocean with the aid of a B.E.L.L. 3.4 , an ultra-sophisticated talking robot diving bell which could utilise its powerful floodlights to illuminate any area of seabed that may be the scene of criminal activity. Pilot episode 'Trawler Trouble' centred on Falcon's attempts to thwart an international gang of cod thieves, and featured a guest appearance from Tim Curry as a deranged Norwegian fisherman who kills a whale by convincing it to swallow a gigantic sack of salt.

Bathysphere P.I. ran for three highly successful seasons until network bosses became doubtful over the third series' tense finale, involving an old car being pushed off the back of a boat, and a man in a cowboy hat getting electrocuted by an eel. Falcon himself was never killed off, and recently fans held an online campaign to bring the series back – but this time set on the moon, called something completely different, and minus Reinhold.

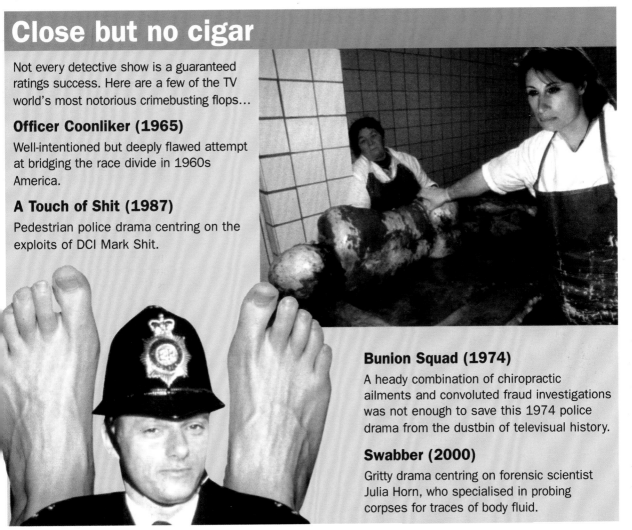

Close but no cigar

Not every detective show is a guaranteed ratings success. Here are a few of the TV world's most notorious crimebusting flops...

Officer Coonliker (1965)

Well-intentioned but deeply flawed attempt at bridging the race divide in 1960s America.

A Touch of Shit (1987)

Pedestrian police drama centring on the exploits of DCI Mark Shit.

Bunion Squad (1974)

A heady combination of chiropractic ailments and convoluted fraud investigations was not enough to save this 1974 police drama from the dustbin of televisual history.

Swabber (2000)

Gritty drama centring on forensic scientist Julia Horn, who specialised in probing corpses for traces of body fluid.

SATURDAY

TV Terrestrial

Licenced to Hill: mound enthusiast Alan Timwell drinks a beaker full of liquidised hill in Hills, Hills, Hills

Worthy Gawps

Hills, Hills, Hills
7.00pm TVGH 2

When the Grand Old Duke of York marched 10,000 soldiers to the top of a hill, critics hit back with a witheringly sarcastic nursery rhyme. Now, almost thirty years later, tors and mounts are all the rage, and the public's thirst for anything hill-related seems unquenchable – quite literally, in the case of Alan Timwell, a 34-year-old graphic designer from Ayrshire.

Timwell drinks liquidised hills: gigantic knolls of soil and turf squashed to the size of a horse's fist and pulped to froth in a specially-designed turbine blender housed in his loft.

'It's like a sort of furry espresso,' he beams, downing a pint glass containing the compressed sod of Saunderson's Mount, an 80ft hillock originally situated outside the village of Yenton Salome in Staffordshire, in its entirety. 'It's not the taste that's the

satisfying thing, although that's fantastic of course,' he claims. 'The real thrill comes from knowing you've put an entire hill inside you.' Quite. Sadly, the smile conceals an impending tragedy. Two days after filming, he choked to death on a bus-sized chunk of granite while attempting to drink both of Oxfordshire's infamous Whittenham Clumps. It's a sobering start to a series of programmes aimed at Britain's growing band of hill enthusiasts: the creators promise to serve up a diet of 'nothing but 100% hill action, bar the occasional peep at a ditch.' Alan would have loved it.

Blanche Formica

Mick Hucknall's Pink Pancakes
11.40pm TVGH 1

The world of pop might seem a million miles away from the world of scrotal flattening – but try telling that to Mick Hucknall. In his new series, starting tonight,

he sets out on a global quest to flatten his testicular sac against as many different transparent surfaces as possible – from the quiet seclusion of his own patio doors, to the nail-biting heights of a glass pod atop the Millennium Wheel. Not that nut-splaying is anything new; at Elizabethan weddings tradition decreed that the groom press his sac against the chapel windows prior to the ceremony, while in 1875 Charles Dickens regaled readers of *Our Mutual Friend* with a 15-page sequence in which Mr Veneering squashes his scrotum against the window of a deep-sea diving helmet in a bid to cheer up a melancholy dairymaid. Ancient practice or not, the sight of a man's testicles spreading across a glass surface like a pair of fried eggs is something that never really loses its magic; consequently this programme manages to be both poetic and touching. And haunting. And short. Bash the phone off its hook and enjoy.

Sara Clock

101 Amazing facts

22. The earliest televisions consisted entirely of rock and were incapable of receiving broadcasts of any kind.

23. In 1978, a bawdy French cartoon called *L'amour Paf!* made broadcasting history by containing the first recorded example of pubic hair rendered in claymation.

24. Dutch entertainment show *Saturday Bang!* recorded the highest number of complaints ever received for a single programme. 13 million viewers contacted the Broadcast Council claiming to have been distressed by a game in which a room full of cats had their tails sheared off by a hypnotised US traffic cop.

TVGH 1

9.00am Get Up and Scream Like a Big Fucking Banshee

Early morning children's show providing a hyperactive mix of cartoons, pop videos, celebrity guests and intense, sustained bellowing. Includes:

9.10 Gus the Glacier
Barely-animated cartoon fun starring a loveable slab of motionless ice.
2. Full Steam Ahead! Following a spell of clement weather, Gus inadvertently slides one millimetre down the valley.

11.40 The New Adventures of Womack and Womack
Animated series.
4. Die, You Bitches. Bobby thwarts a bank raid by kicking fourteen armed robbers to death.
Producer Ce Ce Peniston Subtitles...888

12.00pm Sport Hole
Presented by Steve Rider.

12.15 Purposeful Striding
From Berwick-upon-Tweed.

1.45 Open-Plan Office Flirting
Recorded highlights of the week's most loaded and lingering glances.

2.30 Nonchalant Foodplay
Live coverage of idle side-salad manipulation from Pizza Express in Oxford.

3.15 Paperback Pagefinding
Fiction fans compete to find their place in whatever book they're currently reading.

4.05 Apocalypse Pavement Fucking from Doncaster
Paul Ross introduces recorded highlights of frantic and senseless copulation taking place in the streets of Doncaster following a false late-night nuclear alert.
May contain shots of hard, glistening penises spewing gummy strings of hot white fat all over the moonlit cobblestones.
Producer Relevant Overhaul Subtitles...888

4.45 Cereal Box Head Tomfoolery News
All the day's news read to a giggling child by Peter Sissons careering round the garden with a cereal box over his head.
Producer Alma Geddon Subtitles...888

TVGH 2

8.00am Boxwatch University

8.10 Impenetrable Diagram Studies

9.05 Astoundingly Tedious Made-Up Phenomena
12. Wristalisation patterns in turbonic rotothynthesis.

9.50 How To Do That Trick Where You Fold Your Tongue In Half Lengthways
With Cat Deeley.

10.25 Nine Facts About Magnesium

10.55 Advanced Nokia Ring Tone Programming
Lesson 3: Baroque Classics.

11.55 Apathetic History
11. Ancient Greece: Woo Hoo.

12.40pm Another Fact About Magnesium We Were Going to Mention Earlier But Weren't Really Sure Whether It Was Important Enough at the Time

2.10 Arse / Elbow Differentiation

1.25 Basics of Marketing
Step 1: Delete your own soul.
Producer Tent Slime Subtitles..888

2.30 New Series Jest-iculate!
A panel of painfully earnest deaf people debate an issue specifically chosen to provoke unintentionally funny sign language for the delight of cruel working-ear viewers.
3. Was Hitler,impotent?
Producer Julian Yamp Subtitles...888

3.35 Lionel Thinkbag
Series of abstract philosophical essays in which Michael Gambon narrates the thoughts of an empty carrier bag wafting gently on the breeze in a supermarket car park.
2. Lionel skips over a puddle and fleetingly contemplates the freedom of liquid before getting snagged on a nearby bush.
Producer Raymond Synapse Subtitles...888

4.20 Lay Out a Dog With One Punch
Mark Lawson and friends take turns trying to stun a hound with their fists.
Producer Seb Cacophone Subtitles...888

TVGH 3

9.00am Obligatory Morning Nonsense
Splurge of early morning rubbish apparently being pumped out by a machine.

9.40 The Ten Tasks of One-Armed, One-Legged Hercules
1. Opening a bag of Doritos while standing in a hammock.

10.15 MACH-3 Strobelight Hen Police
Eye-and-mind-fucking Japanese animation.
Producer Tina Tractorgirl Subtitles...888

11.55 Booty Whoop!
Obnoxious dating game in which an audience of youths from grey, rainy Dunstable are prodded around a lurid studio and encouraged to yelp, holler, and gesticulate like American teenagers, while the hosts – one a dim male model, the other an absurd blonde sporting jeans slung so low you can almost see her clitoris – cheerfully bully them into french-kissing one another.
Producer Tak Plakbak Subtitles...888

1.00pm Exhaustive Football Burblechore
Seemingly endless analysis of recent footballing events, approximately six times less interesting than staring at a plank resting against a radiator for ten weeks in order to see it warp in real-time.
Producer Leon Goon Subtitles...888

3.30 Hokey Cokey
Romantic drama starring Patrick Swayze and Jennifer Grey. Crippled teenager Sandra Heart hates every moment of her time at summer camp – until she meets wild young dance instructor Johnny Packett, a troubled former world Hokey Cokey champion. As an unlikely romance between the pair starts to blossom, Sandra jeopardises everything by secretly entering their names in the annual state Hokey Cokey playoffs...
Johnny Packett......................PATRICK SWAYZE
Sandra Heart.............................JENNIFER GREY
Camp Principal............................JON LITHGOW
Director Hal Lodolly (1986, 15) Subtitles.888

TVGH 4

8.00am 101 Great ZX Spectrum Loading Screens
75. Wanted: Monty Mole.
Producer Mel Croucher Subtitles...888

10.00 Chinaman Falls
David Yip introduces previously unseen footage from the People's Republic showing the natives taking spectacular tumbles from bicycles, troop carriers, and high walls.
Producer Runcible Spoon Subtitles...888

11.00 New Series Nightmare Olympics
New series of malevolent dreamscape athletics.
1. Marathon of Horror. Athletes with weights on their feet attempt to run through a trench filled with glue while a pale skeletal hound with human eyes walks slowly behind them with a menacing gait.
Director John Heck Subtitles..888

1.30pm That Ain't Workin'!
Primitive computer-animated sitcom starring the box-headed removal men from Dire Straits' "Money for Nothing" video.
Producer Mark Knopfler Subtitles...888

2.00 Garcia
Vintage 1960s crime series in which unconventional hippy detective Jim Garcia solves crimes with the aid of the mind-expanding properties of LSD. Bummer on Haight-Ashbury. Called in to investigate the suspicious death of an underground cartoonist, Garcia "drops a trip" and finds himself interrogating the dead man's bones – a question-and-answer session that finds Garcia uncovering hitherto unknowable universal truths about the nature of death and existence, along with a terrifying vision of the murderer's face rotating inside an expanding sphere of multicoloured flame. Music by The Lovin' Spoonful and Jefferson Airplane.
Producer Terry Southern Subtitles...888

REGIONAL VARIATIONS

WALES

6.00pm Wales Now

6.30 Wales Then

7.00 FILM: The Welshman (1982)

GARDEN SHED

2.30pm Trowel Time

4.00 Tee Hee! Dusty Flowerpot

5.30 Isn't That Mike From Next Door?

8.00 Secret Drink: Who's to Know?

6.30pm Thick and strong: feats of strength only the dumbest of mungo-headed cuntwits would try to pull off

6.30pm New Series
The World's Strongest and Stupidest Man

The first of six heats in which muscular dunces undertake a variety of pointless and ill-advised tests of strength in a bid to be crowned the most powerful and least intelligent man in the world. *Stage 1.* The contestants glue their eyelids to a filing cabinet filled with coal and attempt to lift it over their heads without falling over or using their hands.

Producer Salamander Godswipe　　　　*Subtitles...888*

8.00 Plebdazzle Party!

Lowest common denominator high-jinks and feeble-minded pantomime, laser-targeted at overweight proletarian halfwits lolling around on their gaudy sofas, slowly digesting sorry lumpen gutfuls of masticated oven chips, ketchup and Hoof-and-Eyelid Meatlike Grills. This week: to a ceaseless backdrop of loud, tinny applause, a rubbish comedian dressed as an Italian chef topples backward into a custard vat, the host pretends to faint following a peck on the cheek from a leggy lovely, and brains and arteries across the land are once more clogged to choking point with oleaginous dimbo-shit.

Producer Ray Skunk　　　　*Subtitles...888*

9.00 New Series
A Question of Sp-Ow!

New series from the makers of *A Question of Sport* in which contestants answer sporting posers while being randomly poked in the neck with a stick.

Producer Kilgore Trout　　　　*Subtitles...888*

9.30 Tetris: The Miniseries

Dark thriller starring **Nick Berry**.
2. Professor Jack Warburton discovers the source of the tumbling fun to be a shadowy Government bureau, and uncovers the alarming scientific method by which complete rows of blocks mysteriously 'disappear'.

Jack Warburton..NICK BERRY
Hannah Turnpike...CAROLINE CATZ
Spatial Awareness Dude.............................DEXTER FLETCHER
L-Shaped Block..CHARLES DANCE
Cerys Matthews..RAY WINSTONE
Producer Yabadab Ticklebox　　　　*Subtitles...888*

11.40 Mick Hucknall's Pink Pancakes

Fun series in which the world-famous Simply Red frontman flattens his scrotum against a variety of transparent surfaces.
2. Mick practises on a patio door before providing visitors to Selfridge's London department store with an unforgettable window display.

Producer Minnie Stootightomention　　　　*Subtitles..888*

5.50pm How Now Cow PoW: the wartime bovines forced to moo and chew cud in captivity

5.50pm New Series
Fresian PoW

The forgotten story of the many thousands of cows who were injured, killed, or taken hostage during World War II.

Producer Log Nonymous　　　　*Subtitles...888*

7.00 Hills, Hills, Hills

Weekly magazine programme for hill enthusiasts, hosted by John Craven. This week's reports include a look at the controversial new sport of hill-fighting, in which contestants punch hills back into the ground, and an interview with the Lynmouth man attempting to enter the record books by eating six hills with a teaspoon. Plus Konnie Huq's hill news round-up, erotic hill massage tips, hill drinking recipes, and an exclusive behind-the-scenes peek at a frosty moonlit hill.

Director Minnie Wiggins　　　　*Subtitles..888*

8.00 Depressed Citizens Deliberately Dashing Their Own Brains Out Against the Concrete Floors of Shopping Centres

CCTV footage of impromptu precinct suicides performed by ordinary members of the downtrodden populace. This week, the intensely dispiriting Arndale Centre in Wandsworth provides a fitting backdrop as two young shop assistants and a failed businessman hammer away at the unforgiving floor surface like big pink woodpeckers in a desperate bid to bring an end to the unendurable misery of it all. Music by The Vengaboys.

Producer Orwen Allen　　　　*Subtitles...888*

10.30 Cunt

Daily fly-on-the-wall documentary series chronicling the life of Nathan Barley, an upper-middle-class London media prickhole proud to live at the absolute epicentre of a thundering whirlpool of meaningless shit. Today, following a morning spent designing e-flyers for a Six Million Dollar Man fancy dress party on a bleeding-edge Apple Mac shaped like a fucking glass lampshade or something, Nathan meets Jemma for lunch at an All Bar One and receives another cheque from his parents.

Producer Lo-Slung Denim　　　　*Subtitles...888*

11.30 You Be the Phantom

Eerie experimental drama in which viewers at home sit close to their television sets to watch Simon Callow reacting to their reflection as if it were a terrifying semi-transparent apparition intent on murder.

Producer Yamblat Hinks　　　　*Subtitles...888*

3

7.30pm Ha ha! They're dying in flares: Steve Penk chuckles at the amusing tragedies of yesteryear

6.00pm McAllister's Screamboat
Unbelievably irritating US action series starring Lee Majors as river patrol officer Ray McAllister, captain of an experimental eco-friendly police pursuit vessel powered solely by continual high-pitched screaming from its seventeen occupants.
Producer Muggy Bumsrush   Subtitles....888

7.00 Fame for a Finger
Jenny Powell offers a member of the public the chance to star alongside a cast of celebrities in a short film dramatising their life – providing they slice off one of their own fingers with a breadknife beforehand.
Producer Spinn Dizzy   Subtitles...888

7.30 The Best of Seventies Tragedy
Steve Penk introduces clips of disasters and accidents of the 1970s – footage now rendered hilarious by the ridiculous hairstyles, far-out fashions, and dated figures of speech exhibited therein.
Producer Sam Kindaghoul   Subtitles...888

9.30 Film Premiere
Poppa Fuckin' Christmas
Heart-warming tale starring Ice Cube as a tough-talking gangster who accidentally wounds Santa during a rooftop shootout – and is forced to spend Christmas Eve delivering presents in the ghetto while simultaneously evading arrest.
Poppa C..ICE CUBE
Shanice...HALLE BERRY
Cute Foul-Mouthed Kid.............JONELLE CHRISTAPLACK III, JR
Cop Removing Cap, Rubbing Eyes, Saying "I'll Be Darned"........MIKE DUMP
Voice of Rudolph...AL GORE
Producer Seminar Cacophone   Subtitles......888

8.30 Aquatextile Savegoose Challenge
Mystifying gameshow in which contestants don blindfolds and gloves in an attempt to identify a patch of fabric glued to the base of a swimming pool without the use of eyes or fingers, before time runs out and a goose has its head pulled off by a specially-built clockwork machine in front of a party of confused and frightened German schoolchildren.
Producer Butch R. Souse   Subtitles...888

10.00 Inspector Bumhat
Drama series about an aristocratic English detective wearing a Panama hat with a magic backside on the front that erupts in a shower of molten effluence whenever he stands within sixteen feet of an obvious clue.
Producer Glenn Corpes   Subtitles...888

 4

8.00pm A clean romance: Keep Britain Tidy icon Ted Bellingham with starlet lover Minnie Driver

7.00pm Wanking for Coins
Rowland Rivron introduces a new series looking at the world's most desperate and degrading careers.
1. Bestial Porn Fluffer. Rowland chats with a 49-year-old former rock guitarist who works on the set of illegal underground video shoots keeping four-legged performers aroused between takes in exchange for the paltry sum of £1.75 a week.
Do you fellate animals for a living? Do you know how it feels to have a pair of swollen dog testicles bumping against your chin? Has a horse ever fired gallons of thick equine semen down your throat until your stomach swells up like a balloon full of curdled mayonnaise? Would you be prepared to discuss your experience before an openly hostile audience? Our research team would like to speak to you: call now on 020 7946 0007
Producer Des Peratymes   Subtitles...888

8.00 Ted Bellingham Night
Leo McKern introduces a night of programmes saluting the career of Ted Bellingham, iconographic star of the Keep Britain Tidy logo.

8.05 Before There Was Ted
Shocking look back at 1968, the year before Ted Bellingham began his historic campaign. With Britain's parks and pavements buried beneath a nationwide carpet of litter, Prime Minister Harold Wilson declares a state of emergency, and a mob of rioters hurling sweet-wrappers and crumpled soft-drink cans surrounds Westminster demanding action.

9.40 Four Martins and a Martine Down Bellingham Lane
Martin Kemp, Martin Amis, Martin Daniels, Martin Jarvis and Martine McCutcheon relive the moment they first encountered Ted Bellingham on the side of a bottle or crisp packet. Illustrations by Bill Tidy.
Producer Rob Moore   Subtitles...888

10.10 Bellingham
Epic biopic starring John Simm as Ted Bellingham. Despite being born with grotesquely tapered limbs and a gigantic split in his lower back, neckless monochromatic icon Ted Bellingham overcomes both disability and prejudice to unite a nation behind his quest for civic cleanliness.
Ted Bellingham..JOHN SIMM
Harold Wilson...JOSS ACKLAND
Margaret Thatcher...ANNA FRIEL
Scowling Rubbish-Hurling Man........................PHIL OAKEY
Director Milos Forman (1998, 15)   Subtitles...888

1.15am A Tidy Romance
Fly-on-the-wall documentary chronicling the run-up to last August's 'Marriage of the Decade', in which Ted Bellingham and Minnie Driver finally tied the knot, ending months of tabloid speculation.
Producer Paul Gilheany   Subtitles...888

DIGITAL, SATELLITE AND CABLE

MOBVISION

The world's first television network devoted exclusively to the furrow-browed concerns of unintelligent angry mobs.

7.00am Lynchmob A.M.

11.00 Which Pitchfork?

11.30 Britain's Most Suspicious Yet Thus Far Unimprisoned Bachelors
With addresses and maps.

1.20pm 101 Common Placard Spelling Clangers
43: Homasexuals Out.

2.20 He's to Blame: Kill Him
A guide to blinkered knee-jerk decision-making.

3.10 FILM: Frankenstein
Classic crowd-of-dunces action.

5.40 Only Fools and Let's Push Some Shit Through His Fucking Letterbox

6.10 A Question of Brickchucking

7.40 FILM: Death Wish

10.00 Scapegoat 24

AMBULANCE WAITER

The channel for people who dialled 999 over an hour ago but are still awaiting urgent medical assistance.

8.00am Soothing Landscape

12.00pm Scream-a-Long-a-Slasher-Flick
Popular Hollywood horror movies with the heroine's screams removed from the soundtrack, thereby affording agonised viewers at home an opportunity to fill in for themselves.
This week: *Friday the Thirteenth Part II.*

1.00 How Many Fingers?

3.30 Flow-Staunching 101

5.30 Reassuring Footage of Smiling Doctors Claiming Help is on its Way

6.30 BeeBaw BeeBaw

8.00 Stay Awake!
Montage of finger-clicks, thundercracks, explosions and eye-popping hardcore porn, intended as an aid for concussed viewers trying to cling on to consciousness.

11.00 Last Rites

HUH? TV

11.00am Who Wants to Be a Millionaire?

12.00pm Whatever Happened to the Likely Lads?

1.30 Are You Being Served?

2.00 FILM: Who Framed Roger Rabbit?

4.40 Why Don't You...?

4.55 What's My Line?

7.10 Where Are They Now?

9.00 Whose Line Is It Anyway?

10.10 FILM: O Brother, Where Art Thou?

1.25am Car 54, Where Are You?

BOULEVARD HYPERGAZE

Daytime programming for people who want to pretend their television is actually a window overlooking a residential street in an absurdly exaggerated fictional version of Paris.

8.30am French Postman Whistling Frère Jacques

10.15 Clattery, Backfiring Van Driven by Jean Rochefort

11.40 Unshaven Alain Delon Lookalike (Drinking from Champagne Bottle) Saunters Nonchalantly Along Pavement, Doffs Hat in Direction of Unamused Elderly Widow Walking Tiny Pekinese in Opposite Direction

11.50 Feisty Woman in Tight Scarlet Dress Runs After Delon, Shouting and Showing Off Armpit Hair

1.30pm Rubber-Faced Gendarme Pats Head of Cute Schoolgirl Clutching Symbolic White Balloon

2.40 Astoundingly Gallic-Looking Tramp Defecates into Drain

4.20 Scrawny Pigeon Pecking for Baguette Crumbs While Dog Barks

5.00 Top-Hatted, Leotard-Clad Mime Artist Kicks Imaginary Immigrant to Death

6.30 Sunset; Accordion Music

DANGERTAINMENT

Ill-advised feats undertaken live by Hollywood stuntmen and extreme sports fanatics.

7.00am Shark Taunting

9.00 Blindfolded Fire Eating Championships
Live from a balsa wood raft in the middle of a lake of petrol.

11.00 Propeller Licking

1.30pm Cupboardfall
New sport in which participants are locked inside a cupboard full of bowling balls and pushed down a mountainside.

2.15 Wolf Fucking

3.45 Chainsaw Fencing

4.20 Pylon Piss Fight

6.30 Rooftop Stilt Disco
With music by Tavares and the Pointer Sisters.

7.40 Drunken Dentistry

8.10 Anchorchute!
Dangerous skydiving variant with parachutes replaced with a six-tonne anchor.

10.00 Predetermined Russian Roulette
Gun fun with six live rounds and no empty chamber.

11.00 Gangster Cuckoldry

12.30am High Tar Smoking

COUNTRYSIDE INCREDIBLE

9.00am Wow! Rivers!

10.00 Amazing Mud

11.00 Geese and Hens and Ducks and Swans and Herons and Everything

1.10pm Delighted Skyward Pointing

2.15 I Caught a Snowflake!
Phone in your snowflake-catching experiences on 090 755 5555

3.25 Holy Moley, Will You Check Out That Bee?

4.15 Beautiful Shadows

7.30 Dock Leaves!

8.00 Mind-Blowing Straw

8.30 Riding a Bike Past Some Daisies With a Look of Blissful Astonishment on Your Face

9.00 Why Rocks Are Cool
2: Because they just are.

100% STRAIGHT

The channel for straight, poof-hating men who are completely heterosexual and don't have anything against gays but are sick of hearing about them and the things they get up to and don't see why the rest of us have to have it shoved down our throats all the time, and spend most of their time drinking pints of lager and reading about football in the paper and fucking beautiful ladies in the cunt.

7.30pm WWF Heat

8.00 Gays Is Rong

8.15 Classic Rugby League Changing Room Japes

8.45 FILM: Xanadu

10.45 Richard Littlejohn Condemns...
5: Hampstead Heath again.

11.00 Cowboy Aerobics

12.15am Christ, How Can They?
Gay practices described in vivid detail.
Contains diagrams and sound effects and genuine footage of men bending over and spreading their cheeks apart and showing you their holes.

1.10 FILM: Spartacus

2.35 Barracks
Soap set in a cramped modern military base. Sixty new cadets arrive from the teenage training college, forcing the soldiers to double up. Meanwhile the heatwave continues, and the discovery of cannabis leads to a full body search for all the men.

3.05 The World's Most Startling Biological Similarities
3: Male and female mouths.

3.15 In Profile: Geoff Capes

3.20 Fighting Techniques
1. How to Pin Down a Queer.

3.50 Bewitched

4.15 Bloke-to-Bloke
Viewers at home phone in to confirm their own heterosexuality to a panel of gruff male presenters, live on air.
To confirm your heterosexuality call 0907379991

4.50 One Thousand Things You'd Never Do
708: Tongueing another bloke's bell end while gently cupping his lovely balls.

Who's the private eye who's a sex machine to all the chicks? *White Shaft*? Damn wrong

MOVIE CHOICE

5.20pm Just Like a Brother To Me
Bitterly realistic romantic comedy starring **Tom Hanks** and **Meg Ryan**. When stumbling loner John Breaker falls for gorgeous young waitress Katherine Prince, sparks seem set to fly – until she patiently explains to him that while he is welcome to become her best friend, their relationship will never, ever become physical... a theory that proves absolutely correct right up to the day he unexpectedly hurls himself in front of a subway train.
Katherine Prince.............................MEG RYAN
John Breaker....................................TOM HANKS
Unimpressed Coroner..........CHARLES NAPIER
Director Jasper Hutton (1996, 15)

6.45 Clouds: The Movie
Soothing non-drama starring **The Sky** as an ever-shifting panorama of clear blue expanse and swirling fluffy loveliness. Clouds billow across the screen forming vaguely recognisable patterns for several hours, as Tim Robbins provides a relaxing commentary that idly speculates on what the shapes might represent.
Tim Robbins..HIMSELF
Producer Simon Nice (2001, U)

8.20 Carry On Dreaming
Surreal comedy starring **Sid James** and **Joan Sims**. As abstract shape Sid Nanobot drifts through a hallucinatory vista of his own imagining, he encounters a gigantic undulating vagina that controls the flow of time...
Sid Nanobot...SID JAMES
Theoretical Figurine.............................JOAN SIMS
Faceless Oblong.......................................JIM DALE
Voice of the Time Vagina...FENELLA FIELDING
Director Eric Thompson (1962,18)

9.55 Mary Poppins: Paul Ross Soundbite Edition
Popular Disney movie rudely punctuated by meaningless talking head soundbites in which notorious clip show dignityphobe Paul Ross spouts torrents of inane semi-relevant bollocks at the behest of an attractive off-screen researcher. Topics explored at punishing length include *Everyone Remembers Dick Van Dyke's Crazy Accent, Julie Andrews Was "Hot to Trot"*, and *When I Was a Kid I Thought All Nannies Could Fly*.
Mary Poppins.........................JULIE ANDREWS
Chimmerney Sweep...............DICK VAN DYKE
Hog-Eyed Jabbering Sod..............PAUL ROSS
Director Sam Peckinpah (1966, U)

11.25 White Shaft
Action thriller starring **Al Gore** as John Shaft – the compromising, some-holds-barred Caucasian American private detective who once kissed a lady but never used his tongue. Called in to investigate the disappearance of a Harlem mobster's daughter, it isn't long before Shaft has become tight-lipped with minor rage and finds himself forced to write a letter to the relevant authorities.
John Shaft...AL GORE
Director Malcolm Uptight (1999, 15)

1.30am Adults Only Fire Station Jizz War IV
Hardcore pornographic film starring **Mitzi Gorge** and **Buck Socket**. In-between emergencies the crew at Suckwell County fire station engage in sexual encounters and ugly five-way orgies so poundingly relentless your television will soon start to resemble a skillfully animated butcher's window.
Dick Glisten.......................................BUCK SOCKET
Mercedes Drip......................................MITZI GORGE
Joe Nozzle......................................DAMIEN COCK
Susi Plugg...ANUSELLA
Mary Spheres..........................JO INTERCOURSE
Alan Blowhole.....................DAVID COPULATE
Jenny Jiggles..........MARGARET PENETRATION
Lt. Holeslammer........................CHARLES NAPIER
Director Vince Nailer (1994, XXX)

25. Psychologists believe watching programmes containing lots of red makes children prone to hyperactivity. The effect can be counter-balanced by placing a cloth soaked in milk on the back of their necks or kicking them down the stairs.

26. The Spanish equivalent of *Question Time* features 13 naked people smeared in glue, shouting at a picture of a horse smoking a pipe.

27. A 1999 advert for a telecommunications network was banned because it showed the Managing Director flying over Britain in a helicopter, flaking off bits of psoriatic skin onto people's houses and laughing.

19

mobile valhalla

Everything you need for your mobile phone apart from a shield to protect your brain from the radiation

Phone logos to make your plasi-chatbox seem less sterile and impersonal

I ♥ BUERK 2212348	bUmHaT☺ 4453898	WHICH? 80087355	HELP ME 34582012	FUCK OFF 829012812
TWO RONNIES 👓👓 39281023	Despot 92841008	P&O Ferries 00010012	THIS PHONE MAY KILL ME 49281201	UNSTABLE LONER 98100126
FELICITY KENDAL ♥♥♥ 78201823	CHAZ PANTHER 88290126	H U W EDWARDS 78120291	♥ PISSHOLES 88823421	PHIL COLLINS 39239239
☎ THIS IS A PHONE 78201124	MITTEN 71299121	ACORNS RULE! 98921242	WINGS 82349120	♿♿♿ 88911739
DUR UMM UGH DURR 23917321	TED BELLINGHAM 89223171	I'M A WORTHLESS FUCKING IMBECILE 11928118	Jesus' Blood Never Failed Me Yet 34582012	I STAB NURSES 22915015

If you liked those, then your arse will open up like a hydraulic door for these: a picture of a bricklayer whose just discovered his wife's affair with another bricklayer, the amount currently outstanding on your mortgage, an isosceles triangle, two owls having sex in a barn and a pirate crying into a saucepan.

1000's of ringtones to help kickstart any awkward conversation

RINGTONES ▶▶ RECENT CHART HITS

Artist	Title	Code
STATUS QUO	SWEET CAROLINE	23812
CRAIG DAVID	DID IT WITH A LADY	45329
MOBY	THE NEUTROGENA SHAMPOO JINGLE	83833
WILLIAM ORBIT	SONGS OF PRAISE '99	93221
RADIOHEAD	SERATONIN JPEG	45619
THE SOUND OF A	WINDOW BEING SMASHED BY IGGY POP	59201
THE WONDER STUFF	CLAP CLAP CLAP CLAP	93012
MARYLIN MANSON	GOOD GOLLY MISS CARRIAGE	50125
IDI AMIN	HERE COME THE HOTSTEPPER (NOW YOU DIE)	89231
AL THE HOLOGRAM	I'M A FUCKING HOLOGRAM	19348

TOP TV THEMES ▶▶

THEME	MANIMAL
THEME	IT'S GARRY SHANDLING'S SHOW
THEME	YOU FUCKED A MONSTER
THEME	BBC SOUTH TODAY
THEME	JASON AND THE NUTMEG MINE
THEME	SLAMBACK & POKEHOLE
THEME	ROOTS
THEME	CRIMEWATCH
THEME	CRIMEWATCH EXTRA
THEME	DOCTOR TINKLESTICK

CALL 0909 879 0980

... and spend over ten minutes listening to a man wipe his balls down the windscreen of a Land Rover - but only if you're lucky, you might end up listening to the managing director failing to seduce an eighteen year old work experience girl. Call cost £25, an astronomical price for which there is absolutely no justification whatsoever.

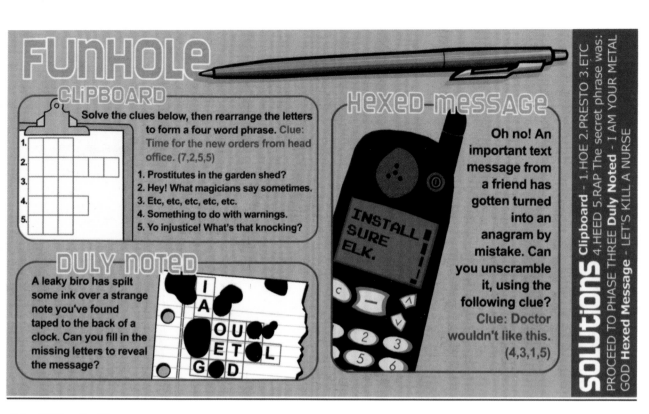

FUNHOLE

CLIPBOARD

Solve the clues below, then rearrange the letters to form a four word phrase. Clue: Time for the new orders from head office. (7,2,5,5)

1.
2.
3.
4.
5.

1. Prostitutes in the garden shed?
2. Hey! What magicians say sometimes.
3. Etc, etc, etc, etc, etc.
4. Something to do with warnings.
5. Yo injustice! What's that knocking?

DULY NOTED

A leaky biro has spilt some ink over a strange note you've found taped to the back of a clock. Can you fill in the missing letters to reveal the message?

HEXED MESSAGE

INSTALL SURE ELK.

Oh no! An important text message from a friend has gotten turned into an anagram by mistake. Can you unscramble it, using the following clue? Clue: Doctor wouldn't like this. (4,3,1,5)

MUTTWORLD

end.

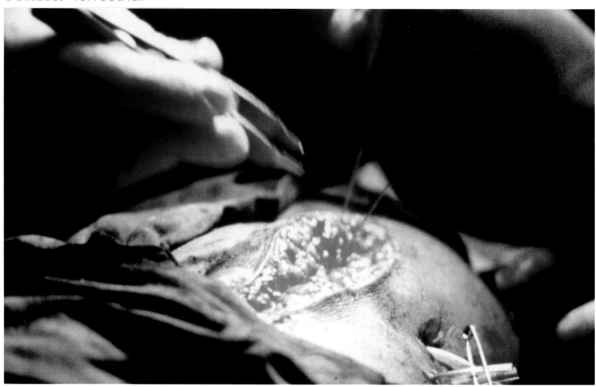

Hands on: get a good grip on some slippery bleeding gutty-wuts in a special interactive *Casualty*

Worthy Gawps

Haywain
7.00pm TVGH 3

Sunday evening means relaxation, and to a TV commissioning editor that spells only one thing: lightweight, mainstream drama with a picturesque setting. Ever since the triumph of *The Darling Buds of May*, programme makers have brought us one bland, easy-on-the-eye serial after another. First there was *Valley Vet*, then *Windermere Midwife*... now the ultimate in chocolate box TV arrives in the shape of TVGH 3's flabbergasting *Haywain*.
Each episode consists solely of a steady shot of the famous Constable painting, accompanied by easy-going narration and occasional bursts of soothing incidental panpipe music. Gentle and occasionally enchanting, the series has only been running for two episodes but already it's proven itself a huge ratings hit.

Inevitably, *Haywain's* popularity has led to a host of cash-ins. Sales of *Haywain* reproductions have gone through the roof, and plans are afoot to build a full-size replica of the scene at Chessington World of Adventures. And the station's rivals have been quick to hit back: TVGH 1 has just commissioned *Goo Goo Lovely*, a series based on the monochrome Athena poster of a shirtless hunk cradling a tiny baby, while TVGH 2 is planning a weekend consisting of nothing but pastel sketches of swans.
But what next for the creators of *Haywain*? Surprisingly, it seems they're about to branch out into high-octane action programming: rumours abound of a forthcoming spin-off series entitled *Haywain's Burning* that will follow the exploits of a team of firemen stationed somewhere behind the watermill.
In summary, then: *ahhh*.
Julie Pissle

Casualty
7.00pm TVGH 1

A unique interactive episode of the gore-packed soap tonight, as Holby fans are invited to take part at home in a bid to enhance the viewing experience.
You don't need any high-tech digital equipment – just a bowl, a cloth, a pair of scissors, and two pounds of raw stewing steak.
The idea is simple – viewers heat the beef in a microwave oven for a few seconds (to bring it to body temperature), then tip it into a bowl in their lap and sit in front of the television.
The episode contains a scene set in an operating theatre, during which an on-screen prompt commands viewers to dip their hands into the bowl and start kneading the warm meat between their fingers, thereby putting you at the very forefront of the action. Neat.
Brian Skonk

28. Imagine the aerial socket at the back of your TV is its equivalent of an anus and you'll feel uncomfortable next time you have to plug the lead in.

29. In Poland, all televisions have round screens and are only allowed to show footage of the ocean bobbing around. Their most popular programmes are *Ship Ahoy* and *Crazy Porthole Hour*.

30. The first recorded occurrence of 'Tube Rage' happened in 1979, when one man for Missouri was so incensed by a plot inconsistency of an episode of *The Dukes of Hazzard*, he murdered his family with a hammer.

TV GH 1

8.00am The Annual Royal Regimental Regiment's Parliamentary Trooping Ceremonial Parade
Downright unendurable live coverage of some ancient monarchical formality of interest solely to idiots, xenophobes and dribble-splattered coffin-dodgers, replete with embarrassingly servile commentary whispered in awe by a Grade-A fuckfaced cunthole. They may as well broadcast footage of a man slowly working a teaspoon up his arse instead. At least that'd be entertaining.
Producer Viscount Yak   Subtitles...888

12.30pm Man Slowly Working a Teaspoon Up His Arse
See? Now that's television. And the look on his face is an absolute picture.
Producer Ivor Cutlery   Subtitles...888

1.30 Bracken Report
John Humphreys introduces the latest developments from the world of bracken.
Producer Relevant Overhaul Subtitles...888

2.30 EastEnders Omnibus
The Queen Vic regulars are in for a surprise when the new landlady turns out to be little more than a stack of rubber quoits with a balloon for a head. Meanwhile, there's trouble for Ian when he accidentally glues his face to Victor Spinetti's thigh.
Producer Insert Pageup   Subtitles...888

3.30 Bus Window Fingersketch News
Today's world events traced in diagrammatic form on a misted bus window by a ten-year-old boy in a *South Park* baseball cap.
Producer Alma Geddon   Subtitles...888

5.45 Apathy in the UK: The Twycross Files
4. Although clearly aroused, Pebbles the Chimp seems slightly sad, and can't even summon the energy to lie down and gently fuck the floor.
Producer Log Nonymous   Subtitles...888

TV GH 2

8.00am Sunday Morning Staring Party
Programming for younger viewers, introduced by Heather Mills and Maurice Bendrix from Graham Greene's *The End of the Affair*.

8.10 Newsnight
Animated series based on the popular current affairs programme *I'm Glad You Asked Me That*. Jeremy's interview with the Green Goblin is cut short by news of an immense asteroid hurtling toward the Earth.
Producer Ram Pack   Subtitles...888

9.40 The Magic Noose
Incredibly irresponsible drama series about a group of children who take it in turns to climb upon a stool and poke their heads through a special noose which magically transports them to a beautiful forest filled with chocolate and stardust.
Producer Lamb Atkins   Subtitles...888

10.15 The New Adventures of Womack and Womack
Off-beat animated series.
5. *Hosepipe What?* Bobby is depressed when a state-wide hosepipe ban prevents him from spraying water over a statue of a horse he'd carved from soluble aspirin to impress Aretha Franklin.
Producer Ce Ce Peniston Subtitles...888

1.30pm Bracken Today
Up-to-the-minute look at undergrowth and shrubbery, with particular emphasis on bracken. With Jeremy Vine.
Producer Raymond Synapse Subtitles...888

3.20 Tumblesnow Sunday
David Vine finally dismisses all pretence of an interest in skiing, and simply stands in front of a monitor pointing at chucklesome footage of flailing Norwegians going arse over tit down the icy slopes. Music by Robert Palmer.
Producer Seb Cacophone Subtitles...888

4.30 Look, It's A Dusty Old Clock!
Idiots coo at aged timepieces.
Producer Amanda Ten   Subtitles...888

TV GH 3

9.30am Toonawake
Garish crack-of-dawn scribblecast shot at the faces of dribblesome children.

9.40 Parable Wars
Futuristic animation. A backfiring retro-thruster forces RoboMoses to guide the U.S.S. Crucifix into an emergency landing on a mysterious planet whose population is blighted by a plague of locusts.
Producer Damien Thorn Subtitles...888

10.25 Si Les Vagines Pouvaient Voler
Inappropriately-scheduled French animation.
Producer Squint Nixon Subtitles...888

12.25pm The GlaxoSmithKline Gang
Product-oriented advertoonment. When Aquafresh Boy and Captain NiQuitin turn up at Lucozade Liz's birthday party without any presents, it's down to the Flu-Plus Caplets Parrot to save the day.
Producer Shred Jessington Subtitles...888

1.30 Bracken Uncovered
Painstaking investigation into the world of bracken, examining where it grows, how it got there, and who fell into it on a horse riding holiday. Hosted by Trevor MacDonald.
Producer Panda Farm   Subtitles...888

2.30 Elegance vs The Abyss
Poets Tom Paulin and Seamus Heany compete to stop suicidal drunks hurling themselves from a tall building by leaning out the window and reciting life-affirming verse through a loudhailer.
Producer Lounge Deluxe Subtitles...888

4.00 Double Bill
The Ten Tasks of One-Armed, One-Legged Hercules
2. Playing the saxophone solo to Gerry Rafferty's 'Baker Street' while kicking a beachball up an escalator.
4.30 3. Serving piping hot spaghetti bolognese to fifteen socialites on an ocean liner in the middle of a violent thunderstorm.
Producer Pam Ampersand Subtitles...888

TV GH 4

9.00am YouthBox
Teenage programming.

9.15 Big Pop Knucklehead Gurgleprick Questaclock
Game show in which bland boy band members attempt to make it through a fifteen minute interview on a wide variety of subjects without uttering a single entertaining or thought-provoking comment.
Producer T.A. Pussy   Subtitles...888

10.20 Ripe High
Teenage soap opera set on a Pennsylvania campus peopled exclusively by freshly-developed youths with incredible physiques.
Previously transmitted to masturbating security guards and 24-hour garage attendants at 2am.
Producer T.A. Pussy   Subtitles...888

11.30 Schweppes Rep
Gripping drama about a Cadbury-Schweppes sales representative travelling the North-East of England.
3. Peter exchanges a box of out-of-date Double Decker bars for a wholesale credit note, and encourages newsagent Iqbal Ram to move the Flakes to a prominent position on the counter. Music by Robert Palmer.
Producer David Nibblethorn Subtitles...888

1.30pm Don't Look Bracken Anger
Steve Penk takes a sideways look at the history of bracken.
Producer Dick Touch   Subtitles...888

2.45 Bad Day at Dunkirk Gulch
World War II western starring John Wayne and Jack Palance. When Sheriff Eisenhower and Churchill the Kid join forces to track down a gang of SS cattle rustlers, it's the start of an epic adventure that will eventually lead them to a tense town square shootout and/or the Normandy landings.
Sheriff Eisenhower............JOHN WAYNE
Churchill the Kid..............ROY KINNEAR
Helmut the Rustler.........BRUCE DERN
Hitler.............................JACK PALANCE
Director John Ford (1959) Subtitles...888

REGIONAL VARIATIONS

FRANCE
5.00pm Aujourd'hui
6.30 Maintenant
9.00 Zut Alors!
11.30 FILM: L'Amour Formidable
Contains pubic hair.

CAB OFFICE
3.15pm That'll Be With You in Fifteen Minutes
7.00 Hello, Car Service?
9.00 Six Two, Six Two, This is Base
11.30 Post-Pub Pickups
2.00am What Freshener?
Magic Tree vs Feu D'Orange.

1

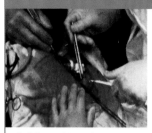

7.00pm Bloody great: writhing guts jerked around for your idle amusement

6.00pm New Series
Do You Think I Give a Fuck? No Really – Look Me in the Eye and Ask Yourself If You Genuinely Think I Give a Fuck. You Can Take Your Pointless Trinkets and Shove Them Up Your Spluttering Shit-Caked Arsehole For All I Care. Now Get Out of My Field of Vision, You Grasping Little Pisscrane, Because Everything About You Makes Me Want to Puke Fucking Blood
Explicitly confrontational version of *Antiques Roadshow*.
Producer Lemonsip Toothpick   *Subtitles...888*

7.00 Casualty
The staff of Holby Casualty are tested to the limit when a demolition ball operator gets a fish-hook lodged in his eye and accidentally knocks a kindly pensioner face-first through a pane of glass into a blazing room filled with lions and razor wire.
Charlie Thingamabob..DEREK THOMPSON
Paraquat Woman..DONNA AIR
Screaming Skewered Man....................................ADRIAN HEDLEY
Epileptic Sword Swallower....................................PAUL SQUIRES
Woman With All Bones Broken and Harpoon Injury.....HELEN SQUAWK
Threshing Machine Disco Dance Blood Clot Dude......DJ FLABPACK
Producer Sick Filth   *Subtitles......888*

8.00 A Hurried Exchange of Phone Numbers
Frank Finlay stars in this two part drama set in a West London wine bar.
1. After noticing his taxi has arrived five minutes early, Peter hurriedly scribbles down his mobile phone number on a napkin and presses it into the palm of a business acquaintance, in the hope he gets invited to a barbeque which some of his colleagues might attend, providing it isn't raining. With John Hannah.
Producer Ray Skunk   *Subtitles...888*

11.00 Mick Hucknall's Pink Pancakes
Mick startles motorists on the M18 by standing on the hard shoulder and performing tricks with clingfilm.
Producer Minnie Stootightomention   *Subtitles...888*

12.00am Blind Viewer Confusion Hour
3. The sound of a television being switched on and off, accompanied by a caption reading "NOT REALLY, YOU DUNDERHEAD".
Producer Blaine Sherrrrrif   *Subtitles...888*

2

5.30pm Face of concern: musical genius Sting pulls compassionate expressions

5.30pm New Series
Sting Cares
1. *East Timor.* New series in which award-winning recording artist Sting takes time out from his hectic schedule to pace the world's troublespots in grainy slow motion, pulling expressions of reflective concern to the accompaniment of tracks from his latest album.
Producer Irwin Allen   *Subtitles...888*

7.30 Cunt
Nathan Barley pushes in front of an unattractive woman waiting at the bar of a recently-decorated riverside pub to order a Stella, a Hoegaarden, and two plates of upmarket bangers and mash for himself and a friend in a faded rowing club T-shirt who excitedly claims to have pushed a finger inside the vagina of a female member of the *Hollyoaks* cast during a drunken clinch in a nightclub corridor the previous night.
Do you and your idiot loudmouth friend deserve to be suddenly and inexplicably killed by a man armed with a hammer, cracking you on the skull right there at the table as you tuck into your snooty fucking pub lunch? Would it give the other diners a surge of nigh-on sexual pleasure to see you slumped face-first in a pile of sweet potato mash with blood bubbling from the back of your head and blending with the onion gravy while your malfunctioning synapses cause your limbs to shudder and pop in a grotesquely comic dance of death? Our research team would like to speak to you: Call 020 7656 7018
Producer Lo-Slung Denim   *Subtitles...888*

9.30 Tasteful Lighting, Monstrous Schemes
Fascinating series of real-time discussions in which sinister committee of powerful businessmen sit around a table and concoct breathtakingly heartless plans, in a setting lit by leading Hollywood art directors and filmed by some of the world's most accomplished cameramen.
1. *The Fate of Christopher Granville.* The group choose an electrician from the Yellow Pages at random and slowly devise a complex plot to have him kicked to death by three of his own children.
Producer Yamblat Hinks   *Subtitles...888*

11.00 New Series
Close the Door on Your Way Out, Dear
Astonishingly cruel series in which women browse through a range of glamorous male models, pop stars, and firemen in a bid to choose themselves a new partner while their current boyfriends look on in dismay from within a soundproof booth.
Producer Razzlecrack Dogwash   *Subtitles...888*

TV GH 3

4.00am Dry mouth: desperate idiots gobble damp bathtowels for bucks

6.30pm Whitney Houston's World War II

Restored archive footage of the Second World War accompanied by a continuous soundtrack of the soul diva's most popular hits, including *My Love is Your Love, It's Not Right But It's Okay,* and *I Wanna Dance With Somebody.*
Producer Muggy Bumsrush   Subtitles....888

7.00 Haywain

Picturesque drama set in Constable's *The Haywain.* 4. From the bank of the stream, a springer spaniel glances at the cart. The horse thinks it might rain.
Producer Spinn Dizzy   Subtitles...888

8.00 Britain's Shakiest Dentists

Hidden-camera footage of accidental oral atrocities and first-hand accounts of agonising incidents recounted by people with fucking big holes in their lips, cheeks and gums.
Producer Jane Reaction   Subtitles...888

9.00 Film Premiere
In the Name of God, Stop Beating My Children to Death with Gigantic Hammers

Made-for-TV movie based on a true story. Amy Sedgwick is an average US mother, until events propel her into a courtroom battle to protect her children from heartless bureaucrats.
Amy Sedgwick..MARY TYLER MOORE
Judge Gavelbanger...KARL MARLDEN
Mikey.......................................RICKY SNIFFLEPLOP III, JR
Susie.................JoBELINDA BRITNEY BRATSHIT IV
Producer Braxal Scrofflewitch   Subtitles...888

11.00 The Ten Tasks of One-Armed, One-Legged Hercules

4. Crossing a rope bridge wearing a big bowler hat made of lead.
Producer Jinks Casey   Subtitles...888

11.30 TV Barfly Buddies

On-screen drinking partners designed to accompany lonely housebound alcoholics. This week, ex-army colonel Samuel Bradshaw-Peters challenges home boozers to match him scotch-for-scotch as he recounts increasingly obscene military anecdotes.
Producer Alfie Collick   Subtitles...888

4.00am Two Hundred Quid for the First Person Who Can Eat an Entire Bathtowel on Camera

Self-explanatory late night game show for the genuinely desperate.
Producer Malcolm Skink   Subtitles...888

TV GH 4

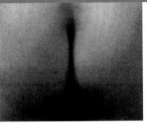

6.05pm Get into the groove: a hard-hitting look at the shadowy world of the arse

5.00pm Cornish Balloon Factory

Fly-on-the-wall documentary series chronicling the lives of workers in a Cornish balloon factory.
Producer Sasha Nixon   Subtitles...888

6.05 Arses: The Truth

Unflinching look at the rarely televised world of human defecation consisting of a single, merciless close-up of excrement emerging from an old man's anus and landing with a thump in a large bowl of flour.
Producer Brian Sewer   Subtitles...888

7.00 Wanking For Coins

Rowland Rivron takes another look at the world's most desperate and degrading careers.
2. Marketing Executive. Tony Warburton has been working in marketing for ten years, and is now incapable of describing a single human emotion without also using the word 'product' in the same sentence.
Do you have an ultimately meaningless job? Have you spent years learning to converse in dense marketing jargon, only to wake one night in a clammy sweat, haunted by the certainty that your life's work improves the lot of mankind not one iota? Do you have an expensive car and respectable income, but no inner life to speak of? Do you sometimes glance at a painting, or hear a piece of music, and fleetingly wonder how it could all have been so different? Can you hear the sound of someone sobbing? Is it you? Our research team would like to speak to you: call now on 020 7946 0007.
Producer Munky Wunky   Subtitles...888

8.30 Art Christ Now

Social commentators discuss contemporary art from within a chrome pod filled with two thousand and one angry wasps. This week, Vikram Seth, Alex James and Frederick Forsythe assess the latest installation by ex-postman Avon Rich, who has tethered a dog to a glass piano in front of a silver machine that fires paint and hot gravel into its eyes whenever it barks.
Producer Matt Pringle   Subtitles...888

11.00 New Series
Nilsen's Twilight Zoetrope

Terrifying new series in which looped reels of rudimentary zoetrope animation recovered from the home of notorious serial murderer Dennis Nilsen are transferred to celluloid and projected onto the backs of unaware pedestrians from an unmarked van slowly cruising Britain's city streets after dark. *Week 1: Hull.* Music by Squarepusher and Jennifer Rush.
Producer Marshall Slavenditch   Subtitles...888

DIGITAL, SATELLITE AND CABLE

NATHAN BARLEY GOLD

The channel that shows nothing but episodes from the life of Nathan Barley, the biggest prick in the known universe.

8.30am Cunt

Nathan Barley sculpts his hair into a messy peak, dons a pair of pedal pushers, and visits a loud, overpriced South London bar to share wood-fired pizza and smug conversation with an equally vile companion.

9.20 Cunt

Nathan Barley rides a tiny metal scooter along the pavement in the direction of an overpriced 'gastro-pub' in order to attend a meeting with a group of worthless toffee-nosed shits intent on setting up an internet radio station with an elaborate Shockwave interface, eternally doomed to be of interest to absolutely no-one other than themselves.

Are you a hideous little posh boy who moved to London and tried to re-invent himself as the epitome of urban cool? Would you do absolutely anything to be considered just 10% cooler than your closest friend? Would you even chop off one of your own fingers? And boil it in blood and eat it? Do you strive to project an air of detached, intelligent amusement while all the time, deep inside you, secretly, something is shrivelling. Withering. Fading out, fading away to nothing... and yet you don't even know what it is? Have you considered giving up? You could just give up. Think about it. No more worrying about trainers or trousers or haircuts. Giving up is simple; open up a vein or two, let the pain flow out of you. Go on. Do it. Do it now. Go to the bathroom. Stare at the mirror for a minute or two. Then grab a blade and slash your arm open. Carve yourself to fucking ribbons. No-one cares. No-one fucking cares about you. Even YOU don't fucking care. YOU'RE AS BIG A SHIT AS YOU THINK YOU ARE. Fancy hacking yourself up on air? Great. Our research team would like to speak to you. Call now on 020 7656 7018

10.55 Cunt

In a crowded, noisy Soho bar, Nathan Barley drunkenly explains to a 21-year-old runner from his brother's video production company that he's written a character based on her into the screenplay of his proposed East End gangster caper, all the time throwing opportunistic glances at her cleavage as his ugly little mouth chews out hollow words and his prick turns stunted trouser-leg concrete.

12.00pm Cunt

Nathan Barley stands in a Soho record shop dressed from head to toe in frighteningly expensive skatewear, bobbing his head loosely in time to an imported hip-hop EP while a malnourished Albanian prostitute half-heartedly fellates one of his schoolfriends in an upstairs flat until he climaxes onto the hem of his £60 Firetrap shirt and instinctively tries to wipe it off with her hair.

Are you being fellated by a foreign national forced into prostitution against her will? Have you contemplated the monstrous sequence of events that led to her current predicament, or are you too busy going 'uhhh' while your cock hops in and out of her mouth like a hyperactive saveloy? At the point where you finally burst, and your ugly little member belches nutfuls of sour, fetid muck across her tear-stained mattress, will it occur to you, even for a moment, that you have directly contributed to the shame-fuelled misery of a frightened and desperate woman? Would you be prepared to re-enact the scene on live television, using a simulated prostitute made from lukewarm mince and pigskin, with musical accompaniment from Shabba Ranks and The Tindersticks? Our research team would like to speak to you: Call now on 020 7656 7018

2.05 Cunt

More candid scenes from the life of Nathan Barley, an odious twentysomething toff and media wannabe who genuinely deserves to die. This week: Nathan spends a king's ransom on a self-consciously 'scruffy' haircut and bags a job as presenter on a new youth-oriented TV show produced by his overpaid womanising uncle.

3.15 Cunt

While visiting the office of a new media design agency run by a schoolfriend, Nathan Barley joins a small group of upper-middle-class twentysomethings as they gather round a monitor to snigger and point at a website displaying photographs of wolves fucking the bodies of mutilated Colombian prostitutes.

4.30 Cunt

Apparently dressed as a Japanese train guard, Nathan Barley sits in a Farringdon bar watching a bootleg DVD full of Eighties porn trailers on a Sony Vaio PCG-F707 laptop nestling on a transparent plexi-resin table containing scattered fragments of depleted uranium and amusing Spanish keyrings.

6.55 Cunt

Nathan Barley is interviewed by Syrie Johnson of the *London Evening Standard* for a feature examining the lifestyle preferences of a group of careerless-but-wealthy freelance twentysomethings – an article which proves so infuriatingly snooty and pointless, it makes anyone reading it grind their teeth with rage.

Do you write meaningless, self-serving features about the dull activities of your worthless fucking friends? Does everyone you know sit around at the fucking Bluebird all afternoon banging on about some non-existent screenplay they're writing, while you knock out page upon page of this nauseating horseshit on a portable fucking iMac? Are you, right now, working on a piece explaining why London's bright young media elite prefer a particular brand of beer, or shoe, or historical figure or something, whereas what you should REALLY be doing is taking a solemn vow to never actually write anything ever again? Our research team would like to speak to you: 020 7656 7018

8.15 Cunt

Nathan Barley lands a regular DJ spot in a pub which used to be warm, smoky, and popular with locals until the son of a wealthy aristocrat turned it into a spacious, brightly-lit catwalk of a building in which loudmouthed members of London's self-appointed young media elite strut about like a pack of trainer-obsessed peacocks, ordering expensive beers and braying insincere, ignorant horseshit at one another over the sound of Nathan's utterly pedestrian mixing.

9.30 Cunt

Worthless upper-middle-class cuntsack Nathan Barley visits the cinema with his friends Susie and Emma to engage in loud, flirtatious banter throughout the film and intermittently scuff the back of your seat with his overpriced trainers.

Are you a loudmouthed little cocksucker with a posh accent who thinks he's some kind of sharp media commentator just because he's sitting in a fucking cinema? Do you and your odious companions consider yourselves faintly superior to everybody else in the building? Can you be heard noisily trading unfunny observations about the film with such relentless frequency that the person in front starts to fantasise about leaping from their seat to knock your fucking head against the wall until it shatters like an egg full of wolf guts? Do you deserve to be kicked about like a rag fucking doll,

all the way down the concrete steps of the fire exit and into the alleyway outside, then left to bleed your last into a puddle of lukewarm dog piss? Our research team team would like to speak to you: call now on 020 7656 7018

11.15 Cunt

Popular docu-soap series chronicling the life of Nathan Barley, the mollycoddled twenty-something upper-middle-class London media shitworker whose very existence is enough to send right-thinking folk everywhere into an apoplectic rage. Having failed to drum up interest in his gangster-caper screenplay, Nathan embarks on a new career as an ironic urban hedonist – drinking, snorting cocaine, having sex with lap-dancers and then writing an incomprehensible monthly column about his tiresome 'exploits' for an overpriced avant-garde lifestyle magazine which considers itself massively influential and important despite two important facts: it sells far fewer copies than *Your Caravan*, and is of interest solely to smug, sneering, moneyed little skunks who are far too busy sliding their fat fucking heads up their fat fucking arses to pay attention anyway.

Are you a cunt? Our research team would like to speak to you: call now on 020 7656 7018

12.20am Cunt

On a humid Wednesday afternoon, while the majority of Londoners are straightening paperclips and nonchalantly contemplating suicide in a hellishly underventilated workplace, Nathan Barley sits before his iMac in the bedroom of his Westbourne Grove apartment, masturbating over a looping MPEG clip of an oriental woman having her face coated by a startling payload of glutinous, HIV-positive semen – and just as his own angry little fleshpipe squirts hot cum into a feverishly oscillating fist, his Nokia 8210 starts chirruping the theme tune to *The Rockford Files*, and within seconds he finds himself conducting an awkward and uncomfortably protracted conversation with his father while a gingerly-balanced cupped handful of watery spunk slowly runs between clenched fingers to drip unpleasantly upon his naked thigh.

Going down in Downing Street: David Seaman plays a priapismic PM in *Disraeli Nights*

MOVIE CHOICE

5.30pm Premiere
Hokey Cokey II: That's What It's All About
Romantic drama starring **Patrick Swayze** and **Phoebe Cates**. Following the tragic death of his wife and dancing partner Sandra in a mysterious boating accident, former Hokey Cokey virtuoso Johnny Packett turns his back on the professional circuit and becomes an embittered recluse – until a young female reporter researching the sinister past of billionaire Hokey Cokey champion Zed Huckledown comes knocking on his door with a broken heart and a pair of dancing shoes...

Johnny Packett...............PATRICK SWAYZE
Marianne Teller.................PHOEBE CATES
Zed Huckledown.....................OJ SIMPSON
Incident-Recalling Guy....CHARLES NAPIER
Speedboat Saboteur..MICHAEL IRONSIDE
Huckledown Henchman #1..RICK GROWLER
Huckledown Henchman #2..MIKE GROWLER
Daily Shieker Editor...................ED ASNER
Hamburglar.................................HIMSELF
Piers Morgan..................JENNIFER BEALS
Urinating Hammer Salesman........................
...................................STEVE GUTTENBERG
Shelf Pointing Dude...................THE ROCK
Duck Grooming Lady................TERI GARR
Director Hal Lo Dolly (1989, 15)

7.15 Corridors of Torment
Horror compendium starring **Christopher Lee**. A prominent psychiatrist is introduced to three patients whose insanity appears to stem from bizarre incidents in their past. In *The Mirror* a young man cleans dirt from a mysterious antique mirror and is horrified to discover the extent of his own sideburns. In *Scary Dog Noise* a woman repeatedly hears a scary dog noise, and in *Oh Now What Was He In?* a couple are driven insane trying to recall where they have seen an actor in a particular television programme before.

Dr Humphrey Sneer....CHRISTOPHER LEE
Director Daralis Crouse (1976, 15)

8.45 Premiere
Stop That Clown!
Manic comedy starring **Rick Moranis** and **Martin Short** as a pair of bungling detectives on the trail of a deranged child molester.

Detective Walter Nash......RICK MORANIS
Detective Randy Wiseman...MARTIN SHORT
Fingers the Clown..........CASPER HAUSER
Director Thomas Jizzlobber (1991, PG)

11.15 Chucklevision: The Movie
Multi-million dollar action comedy starring **The Chuckle Brothers**. When a secret government experiment goes wrong, the hapless pair rocket to four hundred times their normal size and create havoc by wading across the Atlantic to absent-mindedly hurl juggernauts at the Manhattan skyline.

Tall Gangly Chuckle.....................HIMSELF
Small Weasly Chuckle.................HIMSELF
Swearing Official.........................JOE PESCI
Director Ridley Scott (1995, PG)

1.00am Adults Only
Disraeli Nights
Erotic drama starring **David Seaman** as Tory politician Benjamin Disraeli. Exhausted following the reading of the 1875 Artisans Dwellings Act, Disraeli retires to Downing Street for a well-earned rest – but his slumber is soon disturbed by a surprise visit from an inquisitive 17-year-old named Emily Pankhurst.
Contains lascivious glances, improper language, ankles, full-frontal nudity, sideburn-clutching and goal kicks.

Benjamin Disraeli..............DAVID SEAMAN
Emily Pankhurst...CHARMAINE SINCLAIR
Elizabeth Blackwell.......................JO GUEST
Queen Victoria....LINZI DAWN McKENZIE
Bleached Policeman................BEN DOVER
Director Squint Nixon (1997, 18)

31. A 1959 episode of *Hancock's Half Hour* in which Tony Hancock gets drunk and hurls a chair through a bus windscreen was pulled from the schedules at the last minute after a Gloucester man called Tony Bancock got drunk and hurled a bus through a chair windscreen, killing six in his imagination.

32. Spain's most popular television comedian is Jose Bandolvar, who combs his hair into amusing satirical displays.

33. Women were not allowed to appear on TV until 1958, when two broke into a studio during a live show, and stood in front of a camera for twenty minutes.

MAIL FILE
THE FINAL DAYS OF *DAILY MAIL ISLAND*

The Express called it 'evil'. The Times described it as 'the very worst kind of nonsense'. But nevertheless some thought it made for 'rigorously compulsive, intelligent television' (Daily Mail).

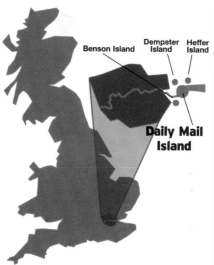

Benson Island
Dempster Island
Heffer Island

Daily Mail Island

This week the largest social experiment undertaken in Britain finally comes to an end. Now the 100 men and women left on a deserted island without access to any form of media other than the Daily Mail, can at long last return to the mainland.

And what a year it's been, all of it captured and fed to the nation in regular episodes of Daily Mail Island. Now, to celebrate the end of the programme, we take a look at some of the characters who have become household names over the past twelve months – and present a special souvenir issue of The Daily Mail Islander, the newspaper the Islanders themselves ran and wrote.

Who are the Islanders?

We profile the Daily Mail Islanders who hit the headlines, and see how their lives have changed.

THEN: Clarinet-playing John and lively Meredith, both social workers, arrived on the island unmarried but accompanied by 3-month-old Mark, Meredith's child by a former partner. 'I love Mark as my own son,' said John.
NOW: John killed Meredith for giving birth to a child out of wedlock, before throwing Mark into the sea at Starkey Point. 'Bastard!' yelled John as he threw the child into the lashing waves beneath. An island court later acquitted him of murder.

THEN: 22-year-old Julian arrived on the island looking forward to forging a new kind of community: 'No cars, no capitalism, no class, just people trying to build a better world for everyone, a world in which we respect nature and use its resources for everyone's benefit' he said on arrival.
NOW: 'It's just too fuckin' boring,' he declared. 'No fuckin' shops, no fuckin' clubs, no fuckin' drugs, no fuckin' clothes, just a load of fuckin' rocks.'

THEN: The Ceku family arrived from war-torn Kosovo hoping to find a peaceful place to provide for their children and find peace.
NOW: The Ceku family were immediately returned to Kosovo after just 6 hours on the island.

THEN: Gay businessman Ivan Smith thought that his financial sense could benefit the Islanders. 'I've a fairly good head for figures and I think one of the first things we need to sort out is a sound economic footing for the island. Then everyone will reap the rewards.'
NOW: Ivan was found dead in his hut, with the word 'Pervert' scrawled on his door. The crime is not being investigated.

Daily Mail Islander

Island Newspaper of the Year   4 Pebbles

The greedy foreign ducks who make a mockery of our unselfish nature

A Daily Mail Islander investigation page 4

15-year-old Sarah guilty of horrifying masturbatory act

DEPRAVED BEYOND BELIEF

Face of the monster

15-year-old Sarah acted "without mercy or compunction".

By **John Upward**

Chief Crime Correspondent

A TEENAGE Daily Mail Island girl has been found guilty of touching her own genitals in a bid to achieve orgasm.

Cheers of "justice has been done" filled the courtroom as the foreman delivered the verdict on 15-year-old Sarah Galoshes, whose mother caught her abasing her own dignity ten days ago at the family home.

As Galoshes wept in the dock, Judge Stephen Hawchurch condemned her as "a selfish, misguided young lady who callously manipulated her own genitalia without mercy or compunction".

Continued on Page 2

Filth: awful, nefarious

Continued from Page 1

The twelve-man jury, which included her own father and several close neighbours, took just eight seconds to reach its verdict.

The public galleries have been packed throughout the nine-day trial, during which Galoshes was ordered to re-enact her crime on a courtroom table, beneath the fixed gaze of the judge, jury, several hundred unappointed court officials, and a sketch artist.

Having found Galoshes guilty, Judge Hawchurch delayed passing a sentence pending the outcome of a public vote intended to decide the 15-year-old's fate. Liberal-minded Islanders suggest we simply accept it and move on, while the majority favour sealing her within a coffin filled with broken glass and dog waste then kicking her off a cliff into the sea.

Outside the courtroom, Sarah's mother, Amanda Galoshes, 39, expressed her dismay at her daughter's crime.

"It scarcely seems believable that a member of your own family could be capable of such a despicable atrocity," she said, choking back tears.

"When they kill her – and kill her they must – I for one will be in the front row, cheering her executioners on, w a t c h i n g through a magnifying lens so I don't miss a damned thing. Death to Sarah Galoshes!"

Despicable: depraved Galoshes dragged fingers across her mimsy.
See Comment Page 5

Second by second... how the wank happened

7.00pm Galoshes family settle down to dinner. Sarah appears calm, normal.

8.15pm Daily pebble count. The Galoshes sit around counting the number of pebbles they have collected that day. Sarah showing first signs of minor irritation.

9.00pm Sarah complains of 'feeling tired' and goes to bedroom.

9.25pm Mother Amanda Galoshes hears 'an unusual noise' emanating from Sarah's bedroom.

9.26pm Mrs Galoshes flings door open to discover Sarah in mid-act.

9.28pm Decency Patrol alerted.

9.57pm Sarah Galoshes admitted to custody.

How should Sarah die?

Cast your vote now and win fifty pebbles for you and your family.
To vote for coffin deathplunge: raise a **BLUE** flag above your dwelling hut.
To vote for accepting it and moving on: raise a **PINK** flag above your dwelling hut.

N.B. Raising a pink flag above your dwelling is a crime punishable by death.

Perzang's Eye

"I hope they kill that little whore"

Do these refugee ducks <u>really</u> deserve our charity?

By **Colin Furious**

IT SHOULD BE THE MOST natural sight in the world. As the sun slowly sets over the village pond, a child tosses handfuls of bread to the ducks. A look of innocent delight spreads across her face as her feathered friends scramble for the crumbs.

But look a little closer and the uncomfortable truth behind this charming tableau becomes apparent. Of the fifteen birds present in the pond, two are immigrants: foreign ducks who flew here from overseas to grow fat on the charity of a blameless toddler.

Ducks on neighbouring islets increasingly see our island as a soft touch: flying here is simple and bread and ponds are rife. Yet once they have arrived, few make an effort to fully integrate themselves into island society. During the construction of the island's sacrificial altar, not a single foreign duck turned up to help out. Most speak no English and have little intention of learning.

Overseas ducks have also been involved in a series of recent disturbances over bread, including the incident in which social leader Miriam Scott received a peck on the finger. Today, reclining in a beanbag in the corner of the communal living room, she rolls her eyes and shudders as she recalls the moment the foreign bird struck.

LITTLE LORD DUCK: how immigrant duck might look if showered with riches instead of bread.

Quacking, flapping, bobbing for bread... the freeloading immigrant wildfowl that exploit our generosity and make fools of us all.

"It looked me in the eye and went for me, just like that," she says. "Later I saw it laying eggs. It's clear to anyone they're coming over here to breed – so they can stay here and eat our crumbs."

Self-appointed duck scrutinising officer Derek Rowlings agrees.

"The floodgates have been open for too long and it's time something was done. They should erect a giant net in the sky so we don't get any more just flying in. And the ones that are here already should have their necks broken by a masked or hooded man, before being tossed into a fire.

"One thing's for certain", he says, shaking his head in dismay at a duck flapping about in the pond, "until action is taken, duck upon duck upon immigrant free-loading duck will continue to pour into our island, laying eggs and gobbling crumbs without a moment's duckish hesitation."

And with that, he snaps the immigrant's neck across his knee. One down. But the question remains – how many more to go?

Daily Mail Islander

COMMENT

A Touch of Evil

Evil Sarah Galoshes has been found guilty of masturbation. It is a verdict no fair-minded person in full view of the facts could argue with.

Her sentence for this motiveless crime – touching herself in the privacy of her own bedroom – is up to the people. Galoshes brought shame on every member of the island with each feverish manipulation of her genitals, so it is fitting that those Islanders should choose her punishment.

Some so-called 'compassionate' Islanders argue we should display leniency towards a 'misguided' teenager, but think for a moment what confusing message that liberal judgement would send out to the young.

Because although we acknowledge that female masturbation is an entirely natural way for a young woman to explore her sexuality, it is still WRONG.

Because although female masturbation may provide a woman with physical pleasure of an intensity she is unlikely to ever encounter with a male lover, it is still WRONG.

Actually, this is probably why it is WRONG.

If we wish to avoid the hideous spectacle of young girls sliding their hands inside the moist crevices of their panties and gently but firmly cajoling their bodies to orgasm, we cannot afford to turn a blind eye.

We must keep the menace of female masturbation in clear view, and remain focused upon it.

In the case of Sarah Galoshes, the verdict has been delivered. Now justice must be seen to be done.

DEATH TO SARAH GALOSHES!

Colour Blind

It appears the remaining three non-white Islanders are still refusing to change colour, in direct opposition to the conformity officials' polite and repeated requests that they do so.

Whilst their frustration at being presented with an impossible demand is understandable, their defiance of authority simply cannot be tolerated.

A society stands or falls on the obedience of its people and their ability to correspond to an accepted norm. No-one wants a world of closed-minded conformity whose inhabitants live in perpetual fear of being condemned as 'different', but that is precisely what we want. Were the disobedience of this trio of criminals to go unpunished, our island would soon find itself quivering at the top of a slippery slope leading to some very hot water at the bottom of a dark and unpredictable abyss.

They must change colour, and they must change colour now.

THIS IS MADNESS

Opinion by **Raymond Blink**

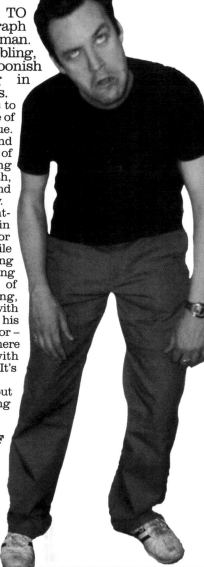

TAKE A MOMENT TO survey the photograph opposite. Look at this man. Just look at him. Dribbling, twirling, pulling goonish expressions, speaking in tongues. This is madness.

He hears voices and claims to be acting under the guidance of a silver android from Prague. He cries intermittently and punches himself on the back of his head. Tongue dangling grotesquely from his mouth, he gets down on all fours and bays like a wolf. What lunacy.

The majority of right-thinking folk do not behave in this crazed manner. And nor would we want to. For while this madman is only too willing to lie on the floor of his living room, assailed by visions of demons – their billowing, gargoyle faces contorted with rage, spitting brimstone into his lap, paralysing him with terror – the rest of us are left to sit here and shake our heads with dismay at this psychosis. It's insane, plain and simple.

Left alone, he may gouge out his own eyeballs, rendering himself blind.

It's madness.

NOTHING SHORT OF MADNESS.

Next week: THIS IS JUSTICE TURNED ON ITS HEAD

The 'fun' craze that wi

Grinning from ear to ear, some play flutes while others dance. Children no older than seventeen laugh out loud as they skim stones across the surface of the lake. In the corner, a couple share an illicit kiss beneath the setting sun. But this is not a snapshot from some faraway decadent hell – it is the reality of everyday life for many teenagers on Daily Mail Island. And it is happening right here and now.

PRISONERS OF FUN: Teenagers leaping like maniacs; their faces grotesquely contorted by 'laughter'

Daily Mail Islander investigates

DANIEL ROBERTSON is only sixteen and has the looks of a young choirboy who couldn't melt butter in his mouth if he clamped a hairdryer to his lips.

His hair is tousled; his childlike eyes bulge with the eager throb of youth. In every respect he resembles the traditional boy next door.

But behind this cherubic appearance lurks an altogether different Daniel – a Daniel who would rather be out having 'fun' than

helping his parents collect and polish pebbles. A Daniel who routinely shirks this and other household duties in favour of aimless pastimes such as skipping, laughing and singing songs aloud. For Daniel is part of the 'fun' scene – the youth movement whose devotees get their kicks from the relentless pursuit of carefree leisure. It is the craze every parent must be aware of -- a fad that is sweeping the island, threatening to tear our world apart and toss the pieces up into the air like existential confetti, then twirl about chuckling as the remnants flitter down

around it like shards of tinsel in a settling snowglobe.

Nonchalantly toying with an illegal wind instrument he claims to have whittled from a discarded chairleg, Daniel smirks as he recounts his recent exploits: lounging on the beach while composing a tune about the sunset, and – most shocking of all – sharing a lingering kiss with a girl he'd met only six days before.

'They're infecting everyone with their actions'

'Her name was Karen,' he says, blithely neglecting to

mention her surname symptomatic of fu seekers' fashion c referring to people b their first names alone i order to imply so-calle 'mutual friendship'.

'We spent a couple c days scouring the beac for seashells, climbin trees, watching clouds,' h recalls blithely, 'and the on the Friday we kissed.'

Just as it seems his stor can grow no mor repugnant, it takes a tur that will appal everyon For it was Karen, h claims, who made the firs move.

'Yeah,' says Danie without a glimmer c shame or remorse, 'it wa really sweet.'

'We were sitting on th old tree trunk taking it i

estroy our youth

...rns to hum (illegal ...ngs) to one another, and ...en she suddenly leant ...rward and kissed me on ...e mouth. It lasted ...everal minutes.'

'The trouble is these ...oungsters genuinely ...on't believe they're doing ...nything wrong,' reports ...r Alan Grover, head of ...e recently-established ...nti-Fun Taskforce ...arged with the task of ...ckling cases like ...aniel's. Dr Grover, ...warded a PhD in Right-...hinkingness by himself ...rlier in the week, is all ...oo aware of the grim ...eality behind the craze for ...un'.

'I've seen it a dozen times ...efore. First they start ...aring at the landscape, ...miling and laughing. ...omeone in the group ...sually starts singing, or –

despite the ban on music – playing an instrument while others – despite the ban on dancing – start to dance.'

'They touch each other'

'Before long you see couples holding hands with each other – which in turn leads to kisses, occasionally involving this area of the mouth,' he says, pointing out a cross-section of a human tongue sketched in coal on the back of a cowskin.

'Once the tongue threshold's been breached it inevitably leads to harder things. I've seen cases in which kids as young as fourteen have touched one another's backsides. There was even

an incident in which a sixteen-year-old girl actively encouraged a boy at least 1.1 times her age to kiss her unclothed bosom. Just thinking about that makes me stiff with disgust.'

Daniel and Karen are not the only victims of the current fashion for laid-back fun. Everyone, it seems, is at risk. Recent statistics indicate that by the time of their eighteenth birthdays, 2 out of every 5 teenagers will have

IN THE GRIP OF THE CRAZE: Twirling a hoop like an imbecile, a young girl surrenders herself to the evil of fun.

How to spot if your child is in the grip of the fun menace

Eyes
Vibrant,
full of life

Mouth
Bent into
'smile' shape

Fingers
Pointing gleefully
at passing clouds

Hands
Often holding
hand of another

Feet
Dancing in time
to woodwind
instruments

Signs every parent must watch for

Danger signals:

Mood: consistently happy and contented.

Relationships: child seems to have plenty of 'friends'.

Behavioural changes: Develops interest in countryside walks, meeting with other teenagers, light-hearted conversation.

Clothing: drab uniform shunned in favour of loose-fitting, gaily coloured garb.

laughed aloud or danced on a beach, and an incredible 1 in 3 will have shared an illegal kiss.

Dr Grover says he cannot be entirely sure how and when the craze began, but he and his colleagues agree the time has come to put a stop to it.

'Enough is enough'

'You could argue that these people only harm themselves,' he claims, 'but they're infecting everyone with their actions.

'After 48 hours studying these 'fun-lovers', I found myself walking home whistling a merry tune about love and marriage going together like a horse and carriage. If that can happen to me imagine the effect it could have on a innocent child.'

The crackdown will start next week. 'We're planning a series of adverts graphically detailing the dangers of 'fun' - once we've worked out what they are,' says the doctor. 'Then we'll erect billboards showing horrific images from wars and famines, to shake some despair into them. And if that doesn't work, the cull will begin. If needs must I will personally shoot these happy-go-lucky souls one-by-one – starting with the handsome musician who had his dirty little hands over that pretty young girl. Yes. And then that blond chap who's always surfing and laughing, he's next. My God, they're going to learn the downside of fun – and they're going to learn it the hard way.'

PIGGYBACK FUN: First step on the road to full genital contact.

Want to stop reading this advert, but can't?

Does your gaze spill across each word with fluid, nonchalant grace?

Find you keep on going, despite your better judgement? Did you consider not starting this sentence only to find yourself unable to resist? Still here and don't know why? Face locked in position, retinas trained on the text like a hawk watching a rodent scamper through a cornfield? Beginning to feel strange, uncomfortable? Hear each word repeated aloud as it forms within your mind?

Feel strongly compelled to submit yourself to its unending flow?

Fill out the coupon below and send it to us, accompanied by a roll of large-denomination bank notes and in reply we will bombard you with a steady stream of similarly mesmerising sentences, word-by-word until the day you die. Now you can remain mildly distracted to the grave! Never feel listless, bored again! Reply today and banish the gnawing mundanity forever!

'Self-appointed people'

Just who do these people think they are?

DAN HETHERINGTON,
Shelter 26

United in agreement

Re: your article 'Is this really the worst thing in the whole wide world?'. My answer would be a heartfelt 'Yes!'

PAUL SIMPSON, Shelter 23

Never forget them

Is this really what people fought in a war for?

IAN LEMINGSTON, Hut 6

Not as good as it was

When I was a child my idea of entertainment was throwing a pebble at a little man made from straw. But it seems boys these days aren't satisfied unless they're playing 'Metal Gear Solid' on a so-called 'PlayStation 2'. What rubbish!

ERNEST MOST, Hut 1

An independent mind

I agree with everything I read.

JANINE NOTTINGHAM,
Hut 72

Let's get him

My neighbour's son looks a bit wrong.

THEO SIX, Hut 9

Really angry

I am furious.

HELEN BRACKETT,
Shelter 2

Now is bad

Things were better in the old days, unless you're reading this several thousand years in the future, in which case it was terrible in the old days, but better in the even older days. If you see what I mean.

DON WASHBACK, Shelter 6

In her place

I am proud to say I have never made my wife come.

LEONARD TELEGRAPH,
Hut 5

A matter of pride

So John Carter (Letters, 16th May) believes we're 'all human'? What rot. I'm sure I speak for many when I say I consider myself first and foremost a Daily Mail Islander. This isn't bigotry – it's a question of pride. Pride in the history of our island and the community we have established here. I for one am sick of being branded a 'racist' simply for suggesting we protect our heritage by repelling all outsiders with clubs and spears and sharpened hoes.

ANDREW CLOT, Cabin A6

Right or wrong?

Homosexuality is a perversion that should be punishable by death

YES

There is no more foul an act of anatomical desecration than homosexuality. Abominable both in concept and in practice, the thought of a man remorselessly driving his penis into my dirty backside is an image that haunts me almost every night.

RICHARD NICHOLSON, Hut 32

YES

I'm fed up of hearing trendy liberals banging on about how it's 'okay' and 'cool' to be homosexual. Anyone who says that must be homosexual themselves – hardly an impartial position from which to approach this sensitive subject.
As a committed heterosexual, I am better equipped to view the issue objectively – and it is obvious to me that homosexuality is wrong.

CARL MILLINGTON, Hut 21

You ask – We answer

Dear Daily Mail Islander,
My friend Bill says the sun rises in the east, but I say it must rise in the west – who's right? There's a ten pound bet on the answer.

JERRY HUGHES, Hut 10

Well, Jerry, you're in luck -- the sun couldn't rise in the east because that's where Japan is. You know: nip land. So the sun rises in the west. Well done, and keep the queries coming.

Straight to the point

■ My husband and I know best about everything.

JACKIE HAMPTON,
Hut 2

■ The young people of today appal me.

DAVID SELWICK-JONES,
Hut 5

■ They say I should stop beating my wife and demanding sex. It's political correctness gone mad.

GRAHAM PIXELPIPE,
Shelter A9

■ No!

LIONEL BOTHERINGTON,
Hut 2

■ Just plain wrong.

MELANIE ABRAHAM,
Hut 33

■ Bad – really, really, bad.

PAUL JACKLIN,
Hut 9

■ I agree with the man who said 'No!' a moment ago.

FRANK STENCH,
Hut 6

Reader's Thoughts

Why not test the validity of asylum seekers' claims by sending them back to the island where they claim they will be persecuted? If nothing happens to them then they are just itinerant scroungers who deserve all they get. On the other hand, if they are tortured and killed, we could welcome them into the country with open arms. We've long had a tradition of being a haven for the persecuted.

JAMES DIGBETH,
Hut 98

Dark-skinned Islanders "refuse to turn white"

TRANSFORMED: How black man might look if authorities are obeyed

THE THREE SURVIVING non-Caucasian Islanders are still refusing to magically transform the colour of their own skin from brown to white despite repeated demands from conformity officials to do so.

"We've tried threatening them, beating them… last week we executed two on the village green as an example to the rest – but they just don't listen," fumed unit leader Michael Tomlinson. "It seems their respect for authority is non-existent."

One of the accused, former locksmith Colin Duncan, is threatening to "beat the s***" out of anyone who tries to enforce the skin tone change. The officials promise further action if their impossible demand is not implemented by 8pm on Saturday.

News in Quick

Gate swings open

■ A GATE beside a field at the top of Seymour's Hill was left open overnight, police say. The gate consists of four horizontal lengths of wood crossed by a fifth, joined at each end by two shorter vertical lengths. It is made of wood. No-one was hurt in the incident, which police are not regarding as suspicious.

Shells cancer fear

■ HOLDING shells to your ear to listen to the sound of the sea may cause brain cancer according to scientists. Crabs and shrimps subjected to prolonged conch-noise were found to perform significantly worse at simple pincer-eye co-ordination tests. The researchers called for all shells to carry warning labels.

Look at her

■ THAT young girl. What is she – sixteen, seventeen? Eighteen at most. All dolled up like a tart in a brothel. This isn't the red light district of Paris. This is Daily Mail Island. Someone should tell her. Making a show of herself like that. Look. You can see her cleavage. Well, you can if you stand on this chair. Blast, I think she's seen me.

LifeSolver

Everyday problems, troubleshot into submission by our experts.

Situation #17:
NO ONE TALKS TO ME AT WORK

Q: Where do you work?

IN AN OFFICE
Probable cause:
You are dull.

Solution:
Try to become less dull. Think up quirky and interesting topics of conversation and write them down in a notebook. Once the notebook is full, start a fresh one. Keep going until you start to build up a library. Spend hours each night scrawling new ideas into your journals. Illustrate them with baffling and intricate diagrams. Do not shave or bathe or change your clothes: keep writing, writing, writing. Hoot! Tee hee! Writey-whitey booky-wooky! Yippee!

ON A BUILDING SITE
Probable cause:
Your co-workers aren't too good at talking and that.

Solution:
Limit conversation to a series of grunts, brusque facial expressions, and ape-like gesticulatory interpretations of the female anatomy.

IN A FAST-FOOD CHAIN
Probable cause:
Conversation amongst worker ants is not permitted.

Solution:
Remember to address the customer with a smile. Keep facing forward, ensuring logo is visible at all times. Choreograph all movements to ensure maximum productivity or face terrible consequences. Extinguish individual mindset. Obey.

IN A LIGHTHOUSE
Probable cause:
You work on your own in a lighthouse.

Solution:
Buy a ham radio kit and hold dull conversations with other throwback nautical loner cunts until your fucking jaw drops off.

Situation #36:
IT'S 2am, I'VE JUST WOKEN UP AND I THINK I CAN HEAR SOMEONE BREAKING INTO MY HOUSE

Q: Which of the following best describes the noise?

INTERMITTENT MUFFLED THUMPS
Probable cause:
Pet or other small animal running around downstairs.

Solution:
If you own a cat or dog that regularly wakes you up at night, consider gluing a small patch of Velcro to your kitchen ceiling. Before bedtime, simply toss the pet upward so its furred back fixes to the tiny synthetic hooks, leaving it to ineffectively twirl its legs all night while you enjoy deep restful sleep.

PERSISTENT, RHYTHMIC KNOCKING
Probable cause:
Sexual activity from next-door neighbours.

Solution:
Dampen their ardour by weeping loudly. If this fails, try picking up a shoe and hammering it against the wall for two hours before wandering outside to hurl rocks and dogshit at their bedroom window.

UNEARTHLY MOANING
Probable cause:
Supernatural phenomena.

Solution:
Remember that ghosts and apparitions are incapable of inflicting genuine injury, while simultaneously steeling yourself for a terrifying paranormal encounter with a howling, gnashing spectre that will alter your life forever.

BREAKING GLASS, FOOTSTEPS, HEAVY BREATHING
Probable cause:
Someone has broken in.

Solution:
Leap from bed as if electrocuted and grab nearest heavy object. Tip-toe to bedroom door and stand stark naked at top of stairs, eyes darting about in the darkness while clammy sweat loosens grip on makeshift weapon. Shout "hey" as gruffly as possible in mistaken belief this will somehow protect you. Gingerly make way to living room, startle petty teenage burglar, and receive frenzied knife blows to head, face, and neck as he panics during escape attempt. Lie on carpet staring at underside of coffee table as lifeblood gurgles from neck wound. Close eyes. Drift toward light.

MONDAY

TV Terrestrial

Fork crying out loud: a day of programmes for people as stupid as this

Worthy Gawps

Downright Average Thick British Viewer Day
All Day TVGH 4

You'd have to be stupid to sit through most of the stuff on TV today – and that's precisely what you are. You only get one life, and most of yours has already been wasted gazing at images put together by people who couldn't care less whether you live or die. Dur, dur: that's you.

Once in a while a quality programme comes along to spoil the flow – but there's no danger of that today as TVGH 4 launches the first of many *Downright Average Thick British Viewer* days – 24 hours of deliberately awful programming devoid of intelligent content. Featuring such highlights as an hour-long broadcast of a shiny coin, and a special reversioned 'Dummies Edition' of *I, Claudius*, the themed day offers something for everyprick.

'We despise our audience', explains channel controller Mick Dicksock, 'simply because they're so jaw-droppingly stupid. 'I'm well aware some viewers might think there's something clever and ironic secretly at work behind *Thick British Viewer Day* – there isn't. It's a bald-faced insult, plain and simple.' Don't miss it.
Isobel Black

Ezekiel's Clockwork Quim
10.00pm TVGH 1

Sailors are notorious for their sexual appetite – but what happens when a man with 'a girl in every port' finds himself adrift in the Atlantic devoid of female company? The solution is obvious, and as far as Victorian inventor Ezekiel Rodican-Brown was concerned, morally repugnant.
Shocked by the near-constant masturbation and sodomy he encountered

during a transatlantic crossing in 1866, Rodican-Brown set about devising an instrument that would relieve the sailor's frustrations mechanically. The result was the world's first clockwork sex toy. It resides in the British Museum to this day, beneath an illuminated six foot sign reading *HEY! CHECK OUT THE METAL VAGINA.*
Today, brass fuckholes are taken for granted, but as this fascinating musical dramatisation shows, their genesis was fraught with difficulties: Rodican-Brown had to contend with almost universal opposition to his work. Society found it hard to accept the prospect of legions of men firing their seed into a cold, hard, whirring cum-jar, until none other than Prince Albert came forward to defend Rodican-Brown's device, sensationally turning conventional etiquette on its head by holding one in his hand and banging it silly during a formal state visit by the Shah of Iran.
Blanche Formica

101 Amazing facts

34. The least successful gameshow ever was Canada's *Who Wants to Hug a Wax Cat?* Not one person entered, watched, hosted, or transmitted the programme.

35. TV actors are often incapable of crying on demand. In order to simulate tears, the producers drill through the back of their skulls and thread pipes through to the tearducts. The pipes are then hooked up to a light water supply.

36. Lap dancers at the Barracuda Bar in Hollywood perform with handheld TVs protruding from their vaginas. Pornographic images are shown on the screens to make their dances doubly arousing.

9.15am Daily Mail Island

Another instalment of the fascinating social experiment in which 100 volunteers from around Britain are 'marooned' on a remote island for a year – without access to any form of media other than the *Daily Mail*.
Day 65. The heterosexuals bury their dead and erect gun turrets either side of the drawbridge.
Producer Dee Stopian   Subtitles...888

10.20 The New Adventures of Womack and Womack

Animated series.
6. Time to Holler. Bobby gets a job winding the village hall clock in the nude – but disaster strikes when his scrotum gets trapped between a pair of gigantic grinding cogs, bursting his testicles like a pair of seedless grapes pressed between the mechanical thumb and forefinger of a vengeful iron god.
Producer Ce Ce Peniston   Subtitles...888

1.00pm Herbie: The Road to Recovery

Sombre sequel to *Herbie Goes Bananas*, following the loveable Volkswagen as he struggles to overcome his recent nervous breakdown.
Director Janet Plannett (1982)

2.50 Light-Hearted Regional News Reporter of the Year

Unrelenting whimsy and cheerful, brightly coloured shirts are the order of the day as hundreds of small-time news journalists specialising in quirky regional stories gather at the Royal Academy for Film and Television Arts for a ceremony celebrating the art of the sideways look at matters of minor colloquial interest.
Awards on offer include *Best Interview With an Elderly Eccentric*, *Most Charming Horse Sanctuary Report*, and *Most Sycophantic Treatment of a Visiting Celebrity*.
Producer Harry Tragic   Subtitles...888

9.30am Animal Zone

A sequence of wildlife programmes vaguely cordoned off to form some kind of notional 'strand' thing.

9.35 Inside Animals
Pinhead-cameras fitted to the heads of drills take you deep inside your favourite animals by boring through their sides. This week: Meerkats.
Producer Mick Caterpillar Subtitles...888

10.00 The Price of Big Tibbles
Sobering computer-generated special in which the makers of *Walking With Dinosaurs* use state-of-the-art technology to recreate the Goodies' famous 'Kitten Kong' sketch, while experts discuss the devastating consequences such a nightmare scenario would have on the capital's social infrastructure.
Producer Graeme Garden   Subtitles...888

11.30 Goldfish Bay
Soap opera aimed at domestic goldfish with a two-second memory span, featuring a comprehensive plot recap every 1.5 seconds.
Producer Bubble Bobble   Subtitles...888

1.30pm Kelly Monteith's Orangutan Airshow
Following a long absence from our screens, the off-beat observational comic returns to host this no-expense-spared travelling entertainment show in which untrained orangutan 'pilots' take to the skies using real aircraft. This week: Kelly's band of flailing primates visits RAF Benson to lead a squadron of Harrier jump-jets up into the wild blue yonder, shortly before hurtling to the ground in a spectacular series of hilarious and deadly high-speed crashes.
Producer Reg Arrows   Subtitles...888

4.30 If Wolves Had Beaks
Theoretical studio discussion.
Producer Coriander Ditch Subtitles...888

5.35 Cow Rambo
Action movie starring a **Cow**. When the Cow Pentagon hears of US cows held captive in Vietnam, cow soldier Rambo is sent in to rescue them.
Rambo................................COW
Colonel Trautman................COW
Dead Gook.........................COW
Director George P. Cosmatos (1987, 15)

9.25am Jakki Shelf
'I Just Can't Stop Sketching Fairgrounds'
Producer Ligament French Subtitles...888

10.15 Moviewreck
Single-minded plugathon in which key scenes from current releases are broadcast sixty-eight times in a row a full fortnight before you can enjoy them properly at the cinema, intercut with superficial autopilot interviews with the cast, pedestrian clips of the director gesticulating to a dumbly nodding Ice Cube, and fun-free footage of some whiny voiced special effects blubberbag in a *Perfect Storm* baseball cap talking us through a wireframe build of the spectacular finale again and again and again and again until the entire sequence is inexorably rendered so mundane and familiar, the experience of finally seeing it up on the silver screen feels more like a lunchtime repeat of *Knot's Landing* than the white-knuckle climax it would have been before the slickarsed marketing fucks responsible for tossing together this say-nothing advertorial assault on your dignity spoiled it all as part of their ongoing quest to bully the world into galloping down to the nearest multiplex to gawp at tits and explosions like the oblivious victims of a dystopian stupidity virus.
Producer Joel Ratzenfuck Subtitles...888

3.45pm The Ten Tasks of One-Armed, One-Legged Hercules
5. Entering a playroom naked and preventing a child from crying.
Producer Jinks Casey   Subtitles...888

4.30 Futile Slo-Mo Visionguess Swindle
Underhanded reality show in which five blind contestants are led to believe they're spending six weeks in a closed apartment trying to guess which one amongst them is a fully-sighted imposter – not realising that in fact, every single one of them is sightless, and that the special Braille clocks they've been supplied with are running at just one third of their correct speed.
Producer Marvin Gag   Subtitles...888

9.00am Downright Average Thick British Viewer Day
A day of undemanding think-o-phobic programming for the Dorito-chugging masses, tossed at the screen by a fat-necked cabal of conceited producers in much the same manner as a smug city prick on a weekend trip to the countryside might disinterestedly sling a handful of cheap supermarket bread at a group of drowsy overfed ducks while casting a listless eye at a nearby fencepost and thinking idly about buying a new car or mobile or computer or *something*.

9.15 Davina 500
Live coverage of the exciting new marathon in which members of the public run from London to Edinburgh in pursuit of a photograph of Davina McCall's face dangling off a stick attached to their own foreheads, earning five pounds for every homeless person they manage to ignore en route.
Producer Text Window   Subtitles..888

11.00 Winkleman Like Budgie
One full uninterrupted hour of Claudia Winkleman tickling, stroking and cooing at a tiny yellow bird.
Producer Legs Howitzer Subtitles...888

12.00pm Shout Court
Genuine legal disputes settled according to which side can bellow their version of events the loudest.
Producer Jennifer Sony
Subtitles...888

1.30 I, Claudius For Dummies
Special edition of the seminal television drama, reversioned to appeal to dum-dums.
1. Derek Jacobi rides a bumper car round and round, intermittently waving at the camera and honking a funny horn.
Producer Lick Bollocks   Subtitles...888

2.00 Pulsing Lights
For you to stare at with your mouth hanging slightly open.
Producer Monk Fish   Subtitles...888

4.50 All About The Aphlabet
Poorly-researched educational series. This week: the letter 3.
Producer Desmond Felt   Subtitles...888

REGIONAL VARIATIONS

GOOSE'S MIND
5.30pm Peck

6.30 Peck Must Peck for Crumbs

8.00 More Pecking

9.00 A Question of Peck

11.30 Inspector Morse

DUNSTABLE
6.00pm Dunstable Eye

7.00 Things to Do in Dunstable When You're Not Dead
1: Get the fuck out of Dunstable.

10.15 FILM: Captain Corelli's Dunstable Mandolin
Reversioned edition of the romantic drama, digitally altered to make it look as if the action takes place in Dunstable town centre.

12.25am Goodnight Dunstable

9.30pm Go to work on a bum egg: viewers compete to curl off the biggest brown plopsy

7.30pm Horse Puppet Disco
Gail Porter introduces a new ground-breaking dance music show in which retired racehorses are transformed into dancing marionettes via a system of wires attached to each hoof, controlled by skilled puppeteers operating an immense mechanical rig. This week: former Derby champion 'Cathedral City' cuts a rug to the sound of erstwhile rave act Altern 8.
Producer Lynn Glynn   Subtitles...888

8.30 Westlife's Nightmare SpoonTomb
Fascinating new series in which the mewling pug-ugly boy band are handed sixty-eight sharpened teaspoons and sealed within a cramped concrete tomb for an indefinite period, in the belief that they'll eventually start to violently attack one another.
Live webcam footage at www.spoontomb.com
Producer Pam Ampersand   Subtitles...888

9.30 Bank Holiday Panblockers
Jamie Theakston introduces a special edition of the show in which viewers email digital snapshots of their own faeces to a panel of celebrity judges. Tonight's bonus prize will be awarded to the first viewer to produce a six-inch stool containing a minimum of ten undigested sweetcorn kernels.
Producer Gia Milinovich   Subtitles...888

10.00 Ezekiel's Clockwork Quim
Musical dramatisation of the true story of Victorian inventor Ezekiel Rodican-Brown and his attempts to perfect the world's first fully-functioning brass vagina.
1. Eureka! During a frustrating six-day trip across the Atlantic, Ezekiel tours the engine rooms and inspiration strikes. Later, at the captain's table, he sketches a rudimentary design for his 'novel solution for concupiscene' on a napkin, and immediately encounters the kind of social opposition that would dog his plan for the next twenty-five years. Includes the songs *Libidinous Vexation is the Curse of Modern Man*, *Deck of Shame*, and *Dreaming of a Mechanised Hole*.
Producer Yenk Benk   Subtitles...888

11.40 Mick Hucknall's Pink Pancakes
Mick joins a group of bucket-and-sponge windscreen-washers by the traffic lights at London's Vauxhall Bridge to offer stationary motorists an unflinching look at his scrotal sac.
Producer Minnie Stootightomention   Subtitles...888

11.20pm Alphabet scoop: use your mobile to make actors yak good

9.00pm Cunt
Nathan Barley perches on a bench in Battersea Park fiddling with the special effects settings on an achingly futuristic Sony digital camera, taking motion-blurred monochrome snaps of his old schoolfriend Crispin, who needs a portrait for the opening page of a website showcasing his own downloadable garage MP3s, and is currently standing in front of the Peace Pagoda, sucking his cheeks in and staring at a tree in the distance.
Do you think you're some kind of fucking Renaissance man just because you've got a few ostensibly creative applications and a shitload of money to spend on high-tech gadgetry? Do you have any idea how many other fuckheads all over the world are, right this very minute, using precisely the same technology to produce precisely the same pedestrian results as you? Why don't you just take all your software, all your gadgets, all your pointless digital fuckery-foo and hurl the lot of it right into the fucking sea? You're using it to churn out shit. Get a fucking grip. You're a cunt; you always HAVE been a cunt, and you always WILL be a cunt – a useless, artless, soulless, worthless, hateful, sickening, handful-of-your-own-shit-fucking cunt-chewing cunt-eyed cunt. And your lazy, delusional stabs at creativity aren't fooling anyone, so stop trying. Prick. Our research team would like to speak to you: call now on 020 7656 7018
Producer Lo-Slung Denim   Subtitles...888

10.00 Buzz Buzz Meadowmouth Vonnegut Assignment
Mesmerising outdoor gameshow in which a contestant tethered to the ground attempts to lick icing sugar from the hind legs of a bee glued to the base of a trowel before a man in a neighbouring field can finish whispering the final fifteen paragraphs of Kurt Vonnegut's *Slaughterhouse Five* into the ear of a slumbering foal.
Producer Tom Lenham   Subtitles...888

11.20 Text Message Theatre
Ground-breaking live drama series in which a cast of actors clutching mobile phones read lines and enact stage directions being sent in by viewers at home.
1. Berlin Encounter. The setting is a German wine bar; opening line is MARY I WANT 2 KISS U, spoken by Sean Pertwee.
Mary (0797 78437)...LISA FAULKNER
Dave (07966 23376)...SEAN PERTWEE
Mr Lindberg (0796648)...TONY ROBINSON
Producer Squint Nixon   Subtitles...888

12.30am Inside Chess
Immersive form of televised chess, where the action is seen entirely from the point of view of the White King, and the commentator speaks from the King's perspective, voicing in particular his scorn for the Black Queen, whom he considers to be little more than a whore.
Producer Lazenby Stripeford   Subtitles...888

TV Terrestrial

3

9.00pm Fuck everything: pissed-off neighbours come to blows

8.00pm Britain's Newsiest Stuff
Populist current affairs programme hosted by Steve Penk and Kirsty Wark.
Producer Sir Royston Fingerwolf   *Subtitles...888*

9.00 Neighbours at War
Series of exploitational televisual investigations into petty disputes involving obstinate middle-class bores and aggressive sociopaths. This week: an unbelievably bitter man from Rochester hurls paper bags full of dogshit at the windows of the family next door while shrieking ugly racist abuse at the top of his lungs and threatening to kill their children.
Producer Len Benn   *Subtitles...888*

9.30 The Bill
DC Jones arrests an unrealistically surly young lad with a faltering cockney accent whom he suspects is actually a tissue-soft upper-middle-class actor currently appearing in a production of *Billy Liar* at the Young Vic.
Producer Nina Neenaw

10.00 The Ten Tasks of One-Armed, One-Legged Hercules
6: *Beating a gazelle unconscious.*
Producer Pam Ampersand   *Subtitles...888*

11.00 Adam Woodyatt's Pringleshit Spincast
Baffling new series in which Adam Woodyatt, playing the moustachioed mascot on the side of a buckled tube of Pringles floating in a green canal, introduces shaky camcorder footage of amateur models defecating onto high-speed turntables inside a starched white tepee.
Producer Nina Neenaw   *Subtitles...888*

11.30 The Metaphor Dimension
Heavy-handed allegorical sci-fi. Rich Man Poor Man. A selfish businessman finds himself being chased through a valley of coins by a giant tramp with his own face.
Producer Bob Sterling   *Subtitles...888*

12.15am The Jerry Springer Show
'I Eat Glass and Kill Dogs and Fuck Handfuls of My Own Shit'.
Producer Alma Geddon   *Subtitles...888*

2.30 Chicken Wizard Tee Hee Hee
Paranormal poultry fun.
Producer Wun Dollar   *Subtitles...888*

4

11.30pm Dur, dur, look at the shiny coin, you sickening bunch of dunces

9.00pm Spoonfed P.I.
Drama series in which smartly-dressed private investigator Ian Spoonfed takes ten minutes to solve a rudimentary crime in which the identity of the culprit is apparent from the very outset, then spends the remaining fifty minutes driving a mid-range Ford Mondeo around some pleasant Cumbrian landscape to the accompaniment of an unremarkable saxophone break.
Producer Felt Desmond   *Subtitles...888*

10.00 Dim Multiplex Livestock Think On Your Behalf
Ground-breaking new public service in which viewers too stupid or distracted to form opinions of their own on contemporary issues are invited to adopt wholesale the attitudes of a random voxpop sampling of outright fucking idiots queuing outside shit Hollywood films. This week: grunting dumbo cow people standing moronically in line for *Scream VII* inarticulately decide your stance on abortion, globalisation, and the human genome project.
Producer Diane Sufferclock   *Subtitles...888*

11.30 Shiny Shiny Coin Coin
Sparkling, recently-polished coin held aloft for you to stare at. Look! Hey there, thicky-thicky bo-bo! Looky-wook at the coiny-woin, you *cunt*.
Producer Lazarus France   *Subtitles...888*

12.00am Midnight Showroom Goonstumble
Two hundred gently guffawing simpletons flail clumsily around the crowded floorspace of a darkened furniture superstore, twirling, colliding and knocking things over while illuminating their snortsome faces with battery-powered torches.
Producer Sod Bottles   *Subtitles...888*

12.30 How it Works: Cutlery
An in-depth guide to using spoons, forks and knives, broadcast in a last-ditch attempt to reduce accidental skewerings amongst the dimwitted viewing public. Contains short sentences, basic visual instruction, and a magic hand that comes out of the side of your television set to thrust a small chocolate treat into your drooping doltish chops each time you nod to indicate you've actually managed to comprehend something.
Producer Phoebe Jeebee   *Subtitles...888*

1.00 Con Air *Twice*
Mindless 1997 aerial prison-break action blockbuster broadcast in its entirety twice in a row.
Good Cop	JOHN CUSAK
Unreasonable Screaming Man	IRISH BLOKE
Shit Villain	JOHN MALKOVICH
Director Jerry Thing (1997, 15)   *Subtitles...888*

MONDAY

TV Terrestrial

43

DIGITAL, SATELLITE AND CABLE

GAWPERS' NETWORK

Programming for those aiming to show off their recently-purchased top-of-the-range widescreen surround-sound home cinema systems.

6.00am Explosions

7.00 Car Chase

7.30 Further Explosions

8.00 Grand Piano Pushed Off the Chrysler Building

9.00 CGI Dinosaurs Fighting Animatronic Robots

10.00 Gunfire

11.00 Three Bonnie Tylers

12.00pm Queen's 'Bohemian Rhapsody' Video Projected onto the Side of an Exploding 600ft-Long Airship

1.00 Gunfire and Screaming

1.30 Boomerangs Ricocheting Off Bells Inside a Hall of Mirrors

2.50 Five Juggernauts Filled with Gigantic Gongs Crashing Into One Another in the Centre of an Ice Rink

3.20 Guns'n'Roses Performing Live On a Stage Dangling Beneath a Superhuey Helicopter Hurtling Through the Grand Canyon Firing Missiles at a Train of Wagons Carrying Ammunition and Fireworks

3.50 Gunfire and Screaming and Tits

4.00 King Kong Throwing a House at the Moon

5.10 B52 Bombers Dropping 25,000 Ringing Alarm Clocks over Vienna

6.50 Arnold Schwarzenegger Kicking an Elephant to Death

7.10 Larger Explosions
With bits of shrapnel flying left and right.

8.50 Gunfire and Screaming and Tits and Foghorns and Strobe Lights and Sparks

9.30 Robocop Taking On 600 Ninjas Inside a Chandelier Factory on the Top Floor of the World's Tallest Building

12.00am Jupiter Colliding with Saturn

12.15 Fresh Fields with Anton Rodgers and Julia McKenzie.

FARMHAND UK

Britain's first channel designed by farmhands, for farmhands.

6.00am Lambing

7.00 Dairymaids Exposed

7.30 Cities Dismissed
4: Paris.

8.00 101 Cruel Barnyard Pastimes
3: Dropping a Breezeblock onto a Calf's Head.

9.00 A Bit of Reed Sticking out of Pond

11.00 Computers for Dummies

12.00pm Haybale News

1.00 A Question of Silage

2.00 Countershriek
An alternative view.
2. Farms are shit.

4.00 EastEnders Moo Plus
Popular soap with additional cow noises dubbed randomly onto the soundtrack.

7.00 Which Goose Egg is Which?
Exciting guessing game.

MASTURBATION MINEFIELD

Erotic reality programming interspersed with offputting imagery in order to turn self-abuse into a game of skill and careful timing.

6.00am When Topless Babes Go Jogging

7.00 Skateboarder Breaking His Leg

7.02 When Checkout Girls Bend Over

7.16 Dying Fish With Hook Stuck in Mouth

8.00 When Clothes Come Off

8.30 Maggots Squirming in an Animal's Eye

8.31 When Knickers Dampen

8.43 Wound Gazing

8.52 When Sex Happens

9.03 Penelope Keith Eating a Garibaldi Biscuit

9.15 When Everyone in the Girls' Changing Rooms Runs Around With Nothing On

10.46 Elderly Man Looking You Straight in the Face

UNNATURAL WORLD OF NATURE

9.00am Zoofights
Crocodile versus Baboon.

10.00 If Shrews Were Huge

11.00 Zoofights
100 Rats versus a Manatee with a Mace on its Tail.

11.20 Diving for Shark Honey

1.00pm Inspector Goose

2.00 FILM: White Rhinos Can't Jump

3.45 FILM: RoboTiger

6.10 How Dinosaurs Cuddled

7.30 FILM: Flight of the Sea-Sod

9.25 Hedgehog Paralympics
From Crystal Palace.

11.10 Buffing the Coelacanth

11.40 Zoofights
Panda versus 10 Badgers.

12.00am Wolf Hospital Live

STAY IN!

8.00am Rush Hour Carnage

9.00 Strangers Kill

10.00 1,001 Potential Outdoor Accidents
37: Railing impalement

11.00 Pollution Update

11.30 Blood on the Pavement

12.30pm Salmonella Cafe

1.30 Haunted Gardens

2.30 Afternoon Slayings That Shook The World

3.00 Mugging, Mugging, Mugging

3.45 Confessions of a Doorstep Rapist

4.30 School's Out: Britain's Most Knife-Wielding Teens

6.00 Why The Sky Hates You

7.00 Twilight Stalkers

8.00 How The Germs From One Fifty Pence Piece Handed Over as Change By a Nightclub Barman Left Six Friends On a Hen Night in an Irreversible Coma

9.00 When Aircraft Fail

10.00 Doogie Howser MD

11.00 Noises In The Street

12.00am Unresolved Hunt for the Mad Midnight Strangler

1LEG 24

The amputee's network.

9.00am Stump A.M.

10.00 Hopper, P.I.

11.00 A Question of Leg

12.00pm Shoe Exchange
Live on-air swapping service for those wishing to trade unwanted shoes.
Left foot call: 090 82833
Right foot call: 090 82834

12.30 FILM: Down On One Knee
Romantic comedy.

2.25 Across Africa With Less Than Two Ankles

3.30 Legs: Eleven
Fly-on-the-wall series following the fortunes of a one-legged football team.

6.30 FILM: Treasure Island

8.20 Changing Leg
Prosthetic makeover show. Lawrence Lewellen-Bowen glues tinsel to a plastic knee.

9.10 FILM: Kilpatrick's Ride
See the Internet Movie Database for details.

10.40 Pro-Am Hopscotch

11.30 Wouldn't It Be Nice To...
37: Wake Up With Your Missing Leg Totally Restored.

IN YO' BRAIN, MOTHERFUCKER

The gangster rap education network.

9.00am Pusher Economics

10.00 Fuckin' Calculus 'n Shit

10.25 Malcolm X: The Merchandising Years

11.15 Glock Physics

12.30pm Great Latin Disses

1.10 Ho Shakespeare
Dick-suckin' bitches re-enact the works of the dead white Bard motherfucker. This week: Much Ado About Jack Shit.

2.30 We Be Slingin' Grammar at Yo' Ass

3.00 One Hundred Words That Rhyme With Fuck
98: Suck.

4.00 Blunted Opera

6.00 Dr Dre's Great Railway Journeys of the World

Up critter creek without a paddle: marsupial survival in *Kangaroo Deliverance*

MOVIE CHOICE

6.00pm Premiere
Kangaroo Deliverance

Harrowing thriller. When four urban kangaroos set out on a weekend canoeing trip along an isolated river, they soon find themselves sailing headlong into a nightmare. Contains pouch violation and marsupial buggery.

Ed Gentry.............................KANGAROO
Lewis Medlock.........................KANGAROO
Bobby Trippe..........................KANGAROO
Drew Ballinger.........................KANGAROO
Director John Boorman (1972, 15)

7.45 Last Play
Bad Lieutenant II: Worse Lieutenant

Uncompromising drama starring **Harvey Keitel**. Contains bad language, full-frontal nudity, drug abuse, nonchalant gunplay, excessive violence, flogging, masturbation, bestiality, auto-fellatio, coprophilia, dysmorphophilia, necrophilia, penile ligation, scrotal infusion, incest, roman showers, docking, dogging, bull-fighting, and a twenty-eight-minute scene in which the corrupt detective slowly pushes a frozen goat's hoof up his arse.

Director Abel Ferrara (1997, 18)

9.15 I Nuh Nuh Nuh Nuh Nuh Nuh Know What You Duh Duh Duh Duh Duh Duh Duh Did Last Suh Suh Suh Suh Suh Suh Suh Summer

Gory horror. A group of teenagers fall victim to a hook-wielding maniac with an appalling speech impediment.

Titsy Cuteass....SARAH MICHELLE THINGY
Jocky Jarhead.......................SKEET ULRICH
Slutty Punkslot................NEVE CAMPBELL
Dweeby Spodfuck..............SKEET ULRICH
Pouty Bigtits......DENISE WHATSERNAME
Director Carson Slaughterhouse (1996, 18)

10.50 Laughing All the Way to the Leeds

Comedy musical based on the popular 1989 Leeds Building Society commercials starring George Cole as a loveable rogue with a 'Liquid Gold' savers account. When a day at the races leaves our hero out of pocket, he concocts an hilarious money-making scheme which soon leaves him 'laughing all the way to the Leeds' once more.

Liquid Gold Man...................GEORGE COLE
Liquid Gold Man's Wife.....ELEANOR BRON
Building Society Cashier....KATE COPSTICK
Director Ron Toss (1990, PG)

12.10am Premiere
Widdleplop Farm

Pointlessly repugnant drama starring Ralph Fiennes. When a lethal gastric virus sweeps through his farmyard, Oxfordshire farmer Harold Walsh soon finds himself standing waist-deep in an ever-growing swamp of pungent manure and musty urine as rivers of diseased molten waste gush from the raw and enflamed anuses of a variety of creatures all over his head, face and neck; hot brown shit dribbling through his hair and into his ears, and even up his nostrils and down his throat like some foul, lumpy, chestnut-coloured soup until he vomits the entire contents of his stomach down his front; bile, milk, and semi-digested Weetabix swirling around with the shit and the piss as he stands there, faint and shaking in the blistering sunshine, mired in the putrescent quagmire of coagulating effluence that now obscures the view for ten stinking, shit-soaked miles.

Harold Walsh...............RALPH FIENNES
Director Peter Jackson (1998, 15)
Return to Widdleplop Farm can be seen on Wednesday at 12.45pm

101 Amazing facts

37. Most televisions are black, in a deliberate move to enrage racists.

38. The Voyager XV space probe contains a DVD full of clips from the most historic moments of television since its inception, including the Moon landing, the killing of Lee Harvey Oswald by Jack Ruby, and Del Boy falling through the bar in *Only Fools and Horses*.

39. It's illegal to transmit footage of a member of the Royal family laughing out loud at the death of a prole. In order to get around the ban, broadcasters must protect the Royal's identity by pixellating their face and replacing the laugh with the sound of a honking goose.

How we used to watch...

TV Schedules from the *TV Go Home* archives

1895

7.00pm Sound Thrashings
Whippersnappers and scoundrels thrashed to within an inch of their lives.
Producer Temperance Withershaw

7.30pm Ally Sloper's Merriment Interlude
After-dinner diversions of a humorous nature with the popular comical character.
Producer Sir Simon Donald

8.00pm A Question of Riding
Around on a Pennyfarthing
Producer Ham Echelon

8.30pm Haversham of the Yard
Haversham investigates the theft of a gold sovereign from a woman of respectable character and finds himself pursuing the wicked ne'er-do-well at the heart of the affair through the streets of London via Hackney Carriage.
Producer Godfrey Conan-Doyle

10.30pm Late Film: Libidinous Enticement
Adult drama. Following the death of her husband in the Tay Bridge disaster, a young widow finds herself short of monies, and is forced to test the bounds of decency by charging common labourers a shilling to glimpse her ankles.
Our audience of highly regarded gentlemen is politely informed that this broadcast contains material of a coarse and bawdy timbre, and as such may be regarded as unsuitable for the gaze of wives or servants.
Producer Micklemuch Wickleward

1941

6.00pm 101 Things to Do With Powdered Egg
67. Hurl it in the bin and sit weeping at the kitchen table.

6.30 Televised Condolences
In a bid to conserve telegram paper, Brigadeer Gerald Ratigan-Thomas delivers heart-wrenching news of fallen soldiers to anxious mothers across the nation, simultaneously wiggling a glove puppet so as not to distress young children.

7.00 Be Prepared
Domestic combat tips which show householders how to defend their home against the Nazis using nothing but everyday implements should a full-scale invasion occur. 13. Mop fencing: the basics.

7.30 GI, Gee Whizz!
Variety show aimed at US servicemen stationed in Britain, broadcast for five fun-packed hours in a desperate bid to distract them from impregnating any more locals.

12.30am Blitzkrieg Improver
Silent footage of exploding fireworks aimed at convincing viewers in the midst of a bombing raid that the terrifying sounds they can hear all around them are nothing but harmless funbursts.

2.30 It's Going to be Okay — It's Going to be Okay
Moving footage of children playing in the fields and men throwing sticks for faithful hounds.

1969

5.30pm The All-New Pink Floyd Cartoon Trip
Impenetrable animated series starring a cast of visual ciphers.

6.00 Swinging Mod Pop Go Yeah!
Humphrey Downing-Street and Joe Carnaby introduce music by Lord Groovy, Neil and the Armstrongs, New Dimension, White Crocodile, Profumo Affair and Betty Pop and the Popettes. The Stanley Matthews Dancers show viewers at home how to do the Castro Four-Step.

7.00 Play for Today: Bloody Bun in the Oven
Gritty drama. 22-year-old Cindy Quant deals with the shame of being an unmarried pregnant single working girl in a monochrome Northern town peopled exclusively by heartless bureaucrats, disapproving neighbours, condescending priests, her own angry father, and Ray Brooks.
Caution: may shake respectable society to its knees.

8.00 Satire-day Night and Sunday More: Ning!
Posh, be-suited Oxbridge graduates poke merciless fun at the very establishment they themselves belong to.
Contains references to Macmillan some viewers may find incomprehensible and tedious.

9.00 The Taming of the Groovy Shrew
Ultra-modern version of Shakespeare's famous comedy.
Petruchio................PETER SELLARS
Katherine................SANDIE SHAW
Baptista................ROY KINNEAR
Lucentio................TONY BENN
Producer Michael Winner

10.45 Stoned Panorama
What is the sound of one hand clapping?

11.15 Slumber Now, Beloved Workforce
A smiling, pipe-smoking Government minister orders the nation's proles to go to bed.

Money to burn: Conspicuous consumption and destruction combine in *The Moneyboast Destruction Gala*

Worthy Gawps

Dance Fatale
1.30am TVGH 3

It's difficult to remember an era in our history when humans didn't dance to express their joy – jigging about, waving their arms and bonding in a common spirit of festival. Ahhh.

But how do people dance when they're – quite literally – being chased around the floor by furious greyhounds? Would they dance at all? You don't think so? Well, what if they were forced to dance, by a masked man who watches from a cherry picker as he rolls dice meaninglessly onto a tin tray? And what if he had a gun, and between licking it and caressing his own biceps, he was allowed to take pot shots at people who weren't dancing with a pre-determined level of pizzazz? And what if there was no end to the show, no winners, no prizes? It just kept going until everyone was either maimed

by greyhounds or shot by the gunman, who, after the programme, would take off his T-shirt and let the dogs drink from his drooling mouth? What would happen then? Well? Well? If you want the answer, you'll have to watch tonight's edition of *Dance Fatale*.

Joey Farrago

The Moneyboast Destruction Gala
7.00pm TVGH 4

If you're one of those people who believes TV brings people together, prepare to eat your words – because tonight it spits on its hands, rolls up its sleeves and steadfastly sets about tearing them apart. For in tonight's *Moneyboast Destruction Gala*, some of the country's richest people can be seen deliberately smashing up luxury consumer goods in front of an audience of paupers.

'They might as well come on and piss on them,' laughs Daz Glow, who had the idea for the show after burning a fifty pound note in the face of a beggar during a night out with friends.

'People have said it's cruel,' he says, idly crushing a top-of-the-range MP3 walkman beneath the heel of his shoe, 'but I say so what? 'Let's face it, you're only going to be offended if you're poor yourself,' argues Glow, reversing a BMW over a trail of Faberge eggs, 'and if that's the case you've probably got more pressing things to worry about than a TV show – such as feeding your kids!'

With the format already sold to the States and a Christmas special in the pipeline in which six chuckling billionaires toss twenty-eight thousand toys into a gigantic incinerator in front of an audience of single-parent families, it looks like *The Moneyboast Destruction Gala* is going to prove hard to ignore. Just like that tramp by the cashpoint machine.

Emma Dove

101 Amazing facts

40. In Albania it is illegal to use a TV remote control after midnight, but for a fee, Greek fishermen will fire long-range handsets from rowboats and change the channels for you.

41. Irish drama serial *The King of Fat Skittles* was filmed through a special camera consisting of a falcon's eye on a stick. Every move the actors made was visible from a distance of 1800 metres.

42. Cornish security guard Morgan Brady became so obsessed with the hit soap *Hollyoaks* that he changed his name to Some Boys Raped Luke, after the show's most controversial story line.

1

 2

TV GH 3

 4

TV GH 1

9.35am Daily Mail Island
Another instalment of the incredible social experiment in which volunteers are marooned on a remote island without access to any form of media other than the *Daily Mail*.
Week 19. Teenage lovers Rowan and Sarah are tied to the beating post with sacks on their heads.
Producer Dee Stopian   Subtitles...888

11.15 New Series
Facepack Avenue
Intriguing new drama series from the makers of *Casualty*. Each week, they follow the day-to-day lives of the residents of Bristol's fictional Facepack Avenue, viewers are invited to guess which of the intertwined sub-plots will culminate in the single facial cumshot that marks each episode's climax.
1. Ben has forgotten Claire's birthday, Simone and Jamie have a bitter argument en route to Mike's garden barbeque, and Lionel's father is interrupted by a surprise visit from a sinister locksmith.
Phone in your cumshot guess on 0901 73758359
Producer Jack Orff   Subtitles...888

12.30pm The Adventures of John Selwyn Gummer
Madcap animated fun with the former minister for agriculture.
Producer Calvin Klock   Subtitles...888

1.15 Britain's Angriest Failures
3. Richard Sandwich from Exeter explains how everything on television is produced by a cabal of guffawing nepotists hell-bent on filling the schedules with simple-minded rubbish, while lying in front of his television smoking cannabis in a grimy towelling robe.
Producer Simon Ragout   Subtitles...888

2.15 Movie Premiere
I Know Snot Poo Flid Arse Bummer
Infantile slasher flick.
Director Hermot Dinks (2000, 15)
Subtitles...888

TV GH 2

9.00am Mind Of The Boatsheep
Animated series detailing the peculiar thoughts that race through the mind of an imaginative cartoon sheep as it rows across a well-known lake.
1. Windermere. The sheep pictures itself climbing inside a gigantic statue of Steve Lamacq to peer from an observation point in his knee at a schooldesk covered in roses. Music by Grandaddy and Kurtis Blow.
Producer Steven D. Wright *Oddtitles...888*

10.20 Who Said That?
Quickfire game show with four hosts and two schizophrenic contestants.
To hear simultaneous auditory hallucinations call 0900 656 7018
Producer Uncle Pigg   Subtitles...888

12.05pm Now That's Regional
Local stories of a minor consequence related by faintly attractive people with off-white teeth.
Producer Pat Ronisingshit Subtitles...552

2.30 Afternoon Movie
Humps For One Mile
Point-and-chortle B-road comedy.
Reg Gearstick.................ROBIN ASKWITH
Minnie Bumper.............JOY FANTAGRAM
Director Sidney Hoof (1975, PG)

3.30 A Question of Do That Again and I'll Smack You
Two teams of athletes answer sporting posers while simultaneously flicking gigantic rubber bands at each other's faces until all bonhomie disappears.
Producer Sue Peeper   Subtitles...888

4.00 University Shitbucket Challenge
Inter-collegiate general knowledge quiz tenuously incorporating a full bucket of human poo.
Producer Mike Mechanic Subtitles...888

TV GH 3

9.25am Jakki Shelf
'Help! I'm Trapped in a Burning Car!'
Producer Ligament French Subtitles...888

10.00 New Series
Centrifuge Bay
Australian soap made entirely on a set housed within a gigantic centrifuge and shot with a camera bolted onto the rotating floor, thereby creating an eerie effect in which the furniture and cast slowly slide away from the centre of the room and wind up hopelessly pinned against the walls at the end of each episode.
Producer Nova Drive   Subtitles...888

12.30pm Molesto the Ape
Illegal claymation.
Producer Arial Black   Subtitles...888

1.45 Boom Goes Lovergirl
Hilarious hidden-camera action as insular nerds spend weeks being led up the garden path by sophisticated androids posing as attractive women, secretly wired to explode the moment the word 'love' is spoken aloud.
Director Melody Nelson   Subtitles...888

3.15 1,001 Petty Compact Disc Irritants
Exhaustive series detailing the myriad frustrations associated with the world's most nonchalantly infuriating storage medium.
23. The little ring of plastic 'teeth' in the middle of a CD case that's supposed to keep the disc in place, but instead contents itself with shattering into a collection of useless see-through granules at the mildest provocation, often before you've even opened the fucking box for the first time anyway.
Next week: those nasty imbecile-beckoning stickers they slap on the front of any CD whose cover art is too subtle to contain the name of the band responsible in huge black type together with a rundown of their hit singles and some enthusiastic quotes from the music press, and which refuse to peel off neatly, leaving behind an ugly patch of gluey sediment flecked with stripes of torn paper slap bang on the front of the thing you've just paid an outrageous amount of money to own.
Producer Jason Lyttle   Subtitles...888

TV GH 4

9.00am Stuff You Won't Need to Know About in Real Life
Needless educational programming.
8.00 Square Roots
8.45 The Difference Between...
3. Aqueous humour and vitreous humour.
9.55 A Taste of Honey by Sheelagh Delaney
10.15 European Treaties
11. The Coal and Steel Treaty of 1951.
11.30 Boyle's Law
12.00pm Oxbow Lakes
1.00 Elements of the Periodic Table
14. Silicon
1.30 Long Division
1.45 Technical Drawing
3. Isometric projection.
2.15 Types of Rock
1. Igneous.
3.00 Rat Dissection
3.25 The World's Slowest Hymns
23. In the Bleak Midwinter
Producer Angela Lamp   Subtitles...888

3.20 Woah! You Mean That Actually Happened?
Tragic events from history re-enacted by actors wearing contemporary street fashion in a desperate attempt to make today's apathetic button-punching youth actually relate in some dim flickering sense to the plight of the blameless souls caught up in the horror of the past.
1. The Persecution Of The Jews. Featuring clothes from Paul Frank, Super Lovers, Hysteric Glamour, Junk, Duffer, Milk Hose, Klepto, Dr Wham, Clitwipe Academy and Sodbox.
Producer Pu Pu Twizzle Subtitles...888

4.45 Cardboard and Piss
Relentlessly grim soap opera. Penny and Steven clash bitterly over household chores. Mike accidentally crushes a child's cat on his way to pick up the results from the hospital.
Producer Gigawatt Leathercot Subtitles...888

REGIONAL VARIATIONS

OIL RIG
6.00pm Rig Talk

7.10 Riggy Riggy Ho Ho
Comedy

8.00 Forget You're Stranded on this Fucking Rig and Keep Staring at this Spiral

TOP SHELF
5.30pm Big Ones

7.00 World's Most Lurid Mastheads

9.00 Smacked Up and Desperate

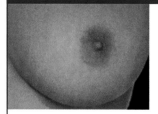

8.00pm Now that's what I call drama: cynical tit exploitation for middle-class lechers

8.00pm Good For The Ratings
Steamy drama. A middle-aged television producer convinces an ambitious young actress to bare all for his latest project. The story is fed to the tabloids, who generate massive publicity by highlighting the explicit nature of the love scenes. On the night of transmission, the actress duly strips, granting the audience a lingering look at her breasts, buttocks, and pubic hair. Approximately one million men masturbate to orgasm in front of the screen before wiping their hands on a towel and phoning for a takeaway.

Overweight Producer..DAMIEN SNEER
Sophie Phwoar...HERSELF
Producer Melvyn Lagg   *Subtitles...888*

9.30 New Series
Congratulations it's a Horse
Off-beat sitcom starring Martin Clunes and Siobhan Redmond. With his prominent city job and beautiful girlfriend, former farmhand Dave Clapton seems to have put his past behind him – until a creature with the head of a teenage boy and the body of a full-grown horse arrives on his doorstep claiming to be his long-lost son…

Dave Clapton..MARTIN CLUNES
Donna Clapton...SIOBHAN REDMOND
Horseboy..JOE ABSOLOM
Social Worker...SALLY PHILLIPS
Aggrieved Farmer...MATT LUCAS
That Bloke From 'Bodger And Badger'... ....HIMSELF
Producer Harry Stockracy   *Subtitles...888*

10.30 Ezekiel's Clockwork Quim
Continuing the musical dramatisation of the true story of Victorian inventor Ezekiel Rodican-Brown and his attempts to perfect the world's first fully-functioning brass vagina.
2. Genesis. Ezekiel works through the night perfecting his design, and solves the problem of tactile chilliness by heating his brass vagina in the fireplace for fifteen seconds. Includes the songs *Cold Metal Lovecave* and *I've Emptied Both Balls Down a Box Warm as Toast*.
Producer La La La Human Steps   *Subtitles...888*

11.45 Snuff-Out Carousel
Celebrity obituary round-up in which poorly photocopied faces of recently deceased household names are stuck to the heads of merry-go-round horses and spun round and round with increasing velocity, eventually creating a strobe-like zoetrope montage of this week's famous dead. Music by Run-DMC and Mogwai.
Producer Mark Scar   *Subtitles...888*

11.00pm Hungry for fame? The stars of Live Aid take a fond look back

9.00pm Cunt
Nodding his head and silently mouthing the words to an Outkast track blasting through his Creative Labs MP3 jukebox player headphones, Nathan Barley bounds up the steps of Old Street Underground station picturing himself in the opening titles of a violent urban thriller, and, lost in this reverie, barges past an exhausted young mother carrying a pushchair, leading her to fire a string of insults at his vanishing back as he cranks up the volume and imagines a sequence in which his twentysomething anti-hero receives a blowjob on an escalator while machine-gunning six policemen coming down the descending side to the toe-tapping sound of 'Caught By The Fuzz' by Supergrass.
Do you stride around while a Walkman fills your head with music, fancying yourself the star of some as-yet-unmade movie? Are you adrift in a narcissistic daydream coloured by the big-name soundtrack of your choosing? Is your life little more than a string of fantasised set-pieces that spool through your echoing cranium, a private cinema of conceited ultraviolent tedium? Reckon your vision could become a celluloid masterpiece? Are you a cunt? Are you? Are you some kind of cunt? Is that what you are? Some kind of cunt? The Kilroy team would like to speak to you: call now on 09034 568 2843
Producer Lo-Slung Denim   *Subtitles...888*

9.30 Waterman's Nest
Occasional series in which Dennis Waterman, dressed as a blackbird, attempts to build a nest in a gigantic concrete tree, while Hywell Bennett clings to his back offering nothing but relentless criticism. Music by Lionel Richie and Fuzzbox.
Dennis Waterman...HIMSELF
Hywell Bennett...HIMSELF
Producer Cillian Mesoft-Lee   *Subtitles...888*

10.30 The Late Review
Mark Lawson and a team of simpering eggheads trade smug observations and brainiac meanderings about the week's cultural offerings while somewhere outside in the darkness homeless refugee children huddle together in the driving rain sucking streaks of hardened birdshit from the iron railings of a nearby fire escape in a desperate attempt to survive.
Producer Ray Diofour-Cunt   *Subtitles.....888*

11.00 After They Were Famous: The Stars of Do They Know It's Christmas?
Seventeen years on, Ethiopian famine victims return to the location of the video shoot to reminisce about their brief moment of fame.
Producer Terry Jerk   *Subtitles...888*

TV GH 3

7.00pm The price of fun: this Faberge egg will be smashed before a pauper's eyes

7.00pm New Series
The Moneyboast Destruction Gala
New series in which prosperous members of the public draw attention to their considerable wealth by buying expensive consumer items with the sole purpose of destroying them in front of an audience of paupers.
1. Computer games company boss Gordon Caudell smashes up a pair of top-of-the-range jetskis using a custom-made hockey stick forged from pure gold.
Producer Pongo Snodgrass   Subtitles.....888

8.00pm Inspector Bell
New series starring David Jason as a detective whose investigations are hindered by his obsessive compulsion to continually ring a tiny brass bell held between his thumb and forefinger in the mistaken belief it will somehow assist the thinking process of those around him.
3. *Ticket to Murder.* During the hunt for a railway killer, the sound of Inspector Bell's relentless tinkling drives three fellow officers to the verge of suicidal despair.
Producer Harry Modo   Subtitles...888

9.00 When Liquids Coagulate
Incredible real-life coagulation caught on camera.
Producer Des Peratymes   Subtitles...888

10.00 New Series
Indiana Jones and the Doomed Office Romance
New drama starring Harrison Ford as archaeologist Dr Indiana Jones, the former adventurer who has turned his back on the world of death-defying peril in favour of the quiet life of a Swinton Insurance call centre manager.
1. Settling into his new desk in Swinton's open-plan office, Indiana glances up from his monitor just in time to spot 23-year-old customer services trainee Karen arriving for her first day at work...
Producer Diddlewop Jiggleknot   Subtitles...888

12.10am The Ten Tasks of One-Armed, One-Legged Hercules
6. *Teaching a deaf boy to dance the hokey-cokey.*
Producer Pam Ampersand   Subtitles...888

1.30am Dance Fatale
The world's most uncomfortable dance show. See today's *Worthy Gawps.*
Producer Charlie Nyhotel   Subtitles...888

TV GH 4

2.00am Whose line is it anyway? Media pricks jerk off in exchange for powder

7.00pm New Series
Choo-Choo Metalface Shinefight Assembly
Eerie gameshow in which contestants dressed as schoolchildren gather on an abandoned railway platform at 3am and take turns shining a torch through the windows of a passing train carriage in an attempt to illuminate the face of a man wearing a featureless metal mask before he can finish carving an unsettling poem onto a wax dummy's chest with an unwashed razorblade.
Producer Lawrence Lennard   Subtitles...888

8.00 Lo-Fi Interactive Night
An evening of conceptually ground-breaking yet technologically simplistic interactivity designed to make the viewer at home feel less like a dumb sack of gawping skin and more like an active participant in the fun-packed 21st century.
8.05 Gent Simulator
Charming experiment in which viewers at home place a hat on top of their television set, then lift it up and down as the face of a kindly old gentleman repeatedly says 'good day to you' on screen.
8.45 Scissors Paper Stone
A televised hand invites you to compete against it in the world's favourite guessing game.
9.15 See How You Like It
Bizarre exercise in household-appliance empathy in which viewers at home shift their television onto the sofa, then stand in the corner while a big pair of computer-generated eyes stare mutely at them for an hour.
10.15 Nationwide Sketch Book
Households across the land are instructed to switch every light in the house on or off according to their location on an onscreen map of the country, in order to sketch out a gigantic comedy penis made of light, visible only from space.
Producer Ham Blastawards   Subtitles...888

2.00am New Series
Wanking For Coke
A cackling camera crew tours the backstreets of Soho in the early hours of the morning, cajoling obnoxious media types into masturbating on camera in exchange for a free line of cocaine.
Producer Alma Geddon   Subtitles...888

4.00 Omen 999
Michael Buerk introduces cheaply-shot VT reconstructions of horrifying accidents from the Omen trilogy.
Producer Damien Thorn   Subtitles...888

TUESDAY

TV Terrestrial

DIGITAL, SATELLITE AND CABLE

ONE-UPMANSHIP NETWORK

8.00am Tennis

9.00 Real Tennis

10.00 Tennis Extreme

10.30 Royal Tennis: Princess Anne vs The Queen of England

10.30 Royal Tennis With Tinsel

11.00 Tennis on the Moon

12.00pm Ultra Fucking Sex Tennis

1.30 Ultra Fucking Sex Tennis Two Times Up The Bum

2.30 Deathmatch Tennis In an Acid Pool from Lourdes

3.30 Tennis: Everyone in London vs Everyone in Paris on a court the size of Wales

4.30 Same As That But Arnold Schwarzenegger is the Umpire

BLAND WORLD

9.00am Don't Children Grow Up, Eventually!

9.30 Kirsty's Best Staircases

10.45 Heterosexual Maths

1.00pm Underwater Fishing

2.30 Mavis Beacon Teaches Typing

3.45 My, You're Quite Tall

4.50 Unsolicited Emails
Read by Bernard Bresslaw.

6.15 We Had Chicken Yesterday
Domestic non-drama.

7.30 Late Shopping
From the Arndale Centre, Leeds

8.40 The World's Shiniest Formica Surfaces

9.00 Mmm, These Doughnuts Are Nice

10.30 Pelmet Talk

11.15 Slightly Changing Rooms

11.45 You Sketch the Duckling
Viewers' sketches of ducklings.

12.15am A Nice Magazine Article About Greek Fishermen at Bedtime

REHASH MOVIEDROME

The premium channel for fans of needless Hollywood sequels and terrible cash-ins.

1.15am Con Air II: Crash Position

2.55 Indiana Jones and the Laster Crusade

4.50 Seven II: The Head Wakes Up

6.30 Star Wars Minus One: Yoda on Campus

8.20 As Good As It Gets Again

10.00 Dial 'N' For Nurder

11.20 Son of Mrs Doubtfire

12.55pm Final Destination: Are We There Yet?

2.20 Higher Society

3.50 How Stella Lost Her Groove And Had To Go And Get It Back a Second Time

5.05 Beyond Roadhouse

6.35 Taxi Driver II: The Perfectly Sane Years

8.00 Another One Flew Over the Cuckoo's Nest

9.40 Wilder Wilder Westest

11.10 Die Hard V: Locked in a Box of Wolves

12.45am Stop! Or My Mom Will Deploy Tear Gas

2.05 Schindler's List II: Hey, There's Some Names in the Margin

3.25 Prick Up Your Ears Again

4.50 Face/Off Episode II: Just The Lips

10.00 Got Carter

11.45 The Other Thing

1.50pm Re: You've Got Mail

2.50 Son of Bride of Frankenstein

10.10 Cheeseburger Hill

3.40 Nil By Mouth: Round Two

4.50 The Very Good, The Extremely Bad, and the Unwatchably Ugly

5.50 Getting Noisier on the Western Front

7.00 High Noon II: High Tea

8.00 White Men Can Jump

KIDCAST EXPRESS

8.00am Bum Knickers

8.15 Arse Bottom

9.00 There's a Man at the Door

10.00 Hairy Willies

10.20 No, You've Got AIDS

11.15 I Can't Find My Other Shoe

11.55 I HATE You!

12.35pm You're Made Out Of Toilet Roll

1.05 Shit Poo Doggy Doo

1.25 I Can See Your Pants

2.40 Na Na Na Na Na NA Na NA NA Na Na NA NA NA NA Na Na NA NA NA NA NA NA NAAAA NAAAAAAA NA NA

3.10 You're Not Playing Properly

3.35 Furry Fanny!

4.00 You Done a Let Off

4.45 Simon Hit Me

5.10 Tail Pull on Mister Cat

5.40 Mrs Broadhurst is Fat

6.10 Don't Want To

6.45 Ice Cream Ice Cream Icy Cream ICY CREAM Ice Cream NAAA Na Na Na Ice Cream Ice Cream Ice Cream Ice Cream

7.30 NO!

8.15 I'm The Prime Minister of the World

8.20 Eeeeeeoooowwwwwn

8.30 Not Going to Bed

8.40 Closedown

PUB DELUSION PLUS

6.00pm Successful Drinkers Throughout History

6.15 Some Joker's Pumping Coins Into the Gambler

6.40 Spin Your Way to Riches: How to Make a Living Playing Fruit Machines

7.30 The Cigarette Diet

8.30 He'll Be Done In a Mo

9.05 Gonna Be Mine All Mine

10.45 Shit He's Had a Win

11.30 Fuck Everything

SPORTHOLE NETWORK

9.00am Carton Opening
Live from Rochester.

10.15 Pro-Am Breathing

12.00pm Workplace Eavesdropper of the Year
All the latest overhearing-who's-getting-sacked-next action, live from an office near you.

1.30 Driftwood Grabbing
Capsized fishermen make frantic attempts to grasp at passing bits of wood. Commentary by Gary Base.

2.45 Font Approval
Live from M2 Graphic Design, Clerkenwell.

3.20 The Nissan Micra Nutbanger 500
Astonishing contest in which a cash prize is donated to the first contestant who can withstand having his testicles slammed in a car door 500 times in a row.

4.40 Sales on Commission
From Dixons in Stafford.

5.15 Tongue Twisting

6.00 Coagulation Playoffs
Week 6: Hot wax versus blood.

6.40 Professional Nit-Picking

7.35 Self-Congratulatory Back-Slapper of the Decade

8.40 Dead Glass Collecting
Live from the Feather and Firkin, Cirencester.

9.20 Unpopped Popcorn Kernal Avoidance
Live from the Warner Village West End cinema.

10.10 Phrase Coining
Stuart Maconie vs A.A. Gill.

11.40 Tug-of-Love Abduction Championships

12.10am Pseudo-Nonchalant Beard Growth

1.55 Neurotic Sexual Fumbling

2.40 Eerie Hooting
Tawny Owl versus Barn Owl.

3.15 Arse Having

4.45 Pro-Celebrity Pointing
This week: pointing at a dog.

5.25 Word Reading
Live from your mind.

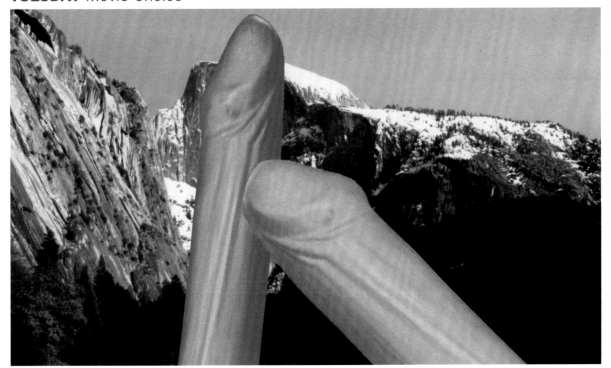

Cock-fighting, 24th-century-style: phallus fencing galore in *Angry Penis Wars*

MOVIE CHOICE

6.00pm Being Mike Batt

Bizarre comedy starring **Lee Evans** as a timid office clerk who discovers he can transport himself inside the mind of 'Remember You're a Womble' composer Mike Batt for fifteen minutes each time he successfully glues a stranger's doorkey to the back of a taxi driver's head.

David Lamp..................................LEE EVANS
Yolanda Lamp........................SALLY PHILLIPS
Lavender Gormenghast...CAROLINE CATZ
Mike Batt...HIMSELF
Director Tyke Jonze (1999, 15)   *Subtitles..888*

7.30 Last Play
Horace Goes Skiing

Slapstick comedy based on the popular Sinclair Spectrum game of the same name, starring **Roy Kinnear** and **Diane Keen**. Abstract blue entity Horace dreams of entering his local slalom contest – but the only ski shop in town lies on the opposite side of an unusually busy road...

Horace...ROY KINNEAR
Ski Shop Lady..........................DIANE KEEN
Ambulance Driver...............PHIL DANIELS
Red Slalom Flag..FRANCES DE LA TOUR
Blue Slalom Flag......................TOM CONTI
Director Mel Croucher (1984, PG)

9.10 Premiere
Logic Problems: The Movie

Animated musical based on the long-running puzzle magazine read by people in hospitals and train carriages, featuring the voices of **Peter Sallis** and **Maureen Lipman**. When librarian Brian Teaser devises a revolutionary problem-solving grid that allows all manner of logical puzzles to be solved in the most efficient manner possible, it isn't long before everyone in town is knocking on his door asking for help with a variety of posers. Includes the songs *Sarah Wore a Crimson Hat But Did Not Arrive By Train* and *Farmer Bunyon's Sheepdog Won The Contest On A Weekday.*

Brian Teaser............................PETER SALLIS
Miriam Teaser...............MAUREEN LIPMAN
Director Steve Bull (1992, PG)   *Subtitles..888*

11.30 Harroween

Offensive remake of John Carpenter's *Halloween* aimed at the Chinese market.
Director Chong Carpenter (1979, 15)

1.10am Premiere
Angry Penis Wars

Action-packed sci-fi blockbuster starring **Matthew Lilard** and **Carmen Electra**. In the year 2355, conventional war is a thing of the past. Mankind settles its differences with televised contests fought by enormous genetically-engineered gladiatorial combat penises in areas of outstanding natural beauty. All is well until a group of exceptionally large and violent battledicks goes haywire during a promotional visit to Yosemite National Park... and it's down to resourceful college student Rip Goodman to save the day.

Rip Goodman.................MATTHEW LILARD
Tippi Heyforth...............CARMEN ELECTRA
Lt Motherfucker............CHARLES NAPIER
Mort Darkboding......JAMES EARL JONES
Director Hampton Wick (1997, 15)

3.15 Jesus Christ Superstar

Jesus, negotiating narrow Somerset B-roads on his Yamaha, misjudges a corner, kills a child during a prolonged skid, then slams into a dustbin and crushes his scrotum.

Jesus Christ, Superstar..ROBERT POWELL
Mary..NIGELHAVERS
Director Godley Motherfucker (1965, U)

43. Cameroon's longest running TV show is the detective drama *Fulani of Lake Chad*. At time of publishing, the show is in its third week.

44. A three-year-old boy saved his mother's life by copying an operation he'd seen performed in an episode of *Quincy*. Two days after her return from hospital he removed her eyes with a teaspoon after watching a documentary on cannibals.

45. It is estimated that by the year 2017 there will be no TV quiz questions left to ask. At this point experts predict that contestants will win holidays, cameras and money by pulling facial expressions.

FUNHOLE

BAD RECEPTION

Which of the receptionists below is the odd one out, and why?

A B C

CLIPBOARD

Solve the cryptic clues below to find out what Gavin from accounting has been sealing his envelopes with. **Clue: Something for your fears?**

1. A cinematic look at guns.
2. New York academy of lycra.
3. Backwards call of the black sheep.
4. Russian station, not Mur.
5. Classics, pick them up from the Geneva contact.

DESIGNERS DILEMMA

You've been asked by a German toy manufacturer to create a logo for a new range of toys… Bearing in mind the client has *specifically requested* the finished design should not be confused with a swastika *in any way*, which of the following designs would you choose?

MUTTWORLD

Chaz Panther's **shocking** new video!

This week's most needless celebrity piddlepuff

£1.35

scorch

INSIDE: WHY THE STARS ARE SO FAB

Issue 12000000

ISBN 1-234-56789-X

9 781234 567897

INCREDIBLE

MARK JEFFRIES' CRATE SNUB

MINNIE DRIVER & TED BELLINGHAM: IT'S LOVE!

EXCLUSIVE!

Robbie Williams hogs front cover!
For sixth week running

News&that

Screen grabs

Dr Harris and Olaf come to blows in *Sodden Swabs*

YOU DIDN'T NEED A thermometer to read the temperature at Prestwich hospital on Thursday – the heat was very definitely on as the ongoing feud between Dr Harris and Olaf finally burst into a face-to-face confrontation. Pointing his finger in Olaf's face, Dr Harris (Mark Jeffries) hurled abuse for ten minutes before turning on his heel and storming out. You can clearly make out the action in this exciting still.

Lucy Frankenstein's boo boo

FORMER KETTLE SWITCH SONGSTRESS LUCY Frankenstein underwent an excruciating ordeal on her new show *Frank Chat Live*, when the autocue failed for five minutes. The look of embarrassment on her face is as plain as day.

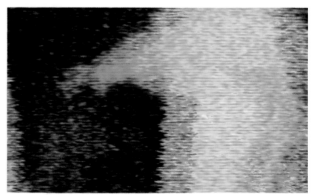

No idea what this is

SUNDAY MARKED THE DEBUT OF PRECISION QUEST, A HIGH-tech sci-fi series filmed using a new digital technique that guarantees DVD-quality visuals. This was the incredible moment when a space banshee attacked the hull of the U.S.S Dominator.

News&that

A Clock & A Cow

A clock and a cow are reportedly dating following an unlikely rendezvous in a Dublin nightclub. "It's tick-tock moo-moo kiss time," said a man in a cap on the wing of a plane.

Tim Vincent & An Operating Manual For A JVC 14" Colour Television

The ex-*Blue Peter* and *Dangerfield* hunk is rumoured to have split from the 36-page black and white instruction manual after 3 months. Pals say Tim never regained the spark he first felt after spotting the stapled booklet in a puddle.

Minnie Driver & Ted Bellingham

Cupboard-faced Minnie fell for the iconographic star of the Keep Britain Tidy logo after spotting him on the side of a crushed sandwich carton clenched between the teeth of a hound. Ahhhh!

Trevor McDonald & Trevor McDonald

Silver-haired Sir Trev recently fell out with himself when a careless glance in a bathroom mirror sparked an argument inside his own brain over whose face was real and whose was merely a reflection. The newsreader's agent has refused to confirm or deny the split, adding fuel to the rumour bonfire.

Not the first

Your Mum & Your Dad

Look! It's your parents. Go on, wave. No don't. It's only a picture. Still, he's your biological father. And she brought you into the world. But who's been romantically linked to your mother in the past? Hmmm…

Your Grandfather

Your dad's dad had a guilty twinkle in his eye the day his son got hitched. And little wonder!

Lord Charles

The upper-crust ventriloquist's dummy has a well-documented fling with your mother during the 1970s.

Everyone in Leeds

Your mother has slept with everyone in Leeds.

The **week** in pictures

Mark walked down the pavement like a man on legs

"And if you look to your right, you can see some red packing crates…"

Wednesday 8th, London

Mark Jeffries walks past some crates

IT'S RUMOURED SOAP STAR Mark Jeffries is about to be written out of hit hospital drama *Sodden Swabs*, but the only thing being sent packing last Wednesday was this pile of crates.

The plastic boxes were stacked high on a London pavement as Mark strolled past on his way to a meeting with his agent – but as far as he was concerned, they were of absolutely no interest whatsoever. He kept his head down as he approached the crates, and barely acknowledged their presence at all, preferring to carry on walking as if nothing had happened.

Quite what Mark's new love, dancer Jane Waterson, will make of it all is unclear. Jane's dad ran a packing crate business for eighteen months, and she may take a dim view of her boyfriend's ambivalence. Let's hope he's as quick to set her mind at rest as he was to walk past these crates.

"…not that I've noticed"

"Dum de doo de doo...
crates? What crates?"

10 Things Ben Affleck Would *Never* Do

1. Sling filth in a dentist's eye

2. Deliberately crash an airship into a school

3. Marry an automated tennis ball serving machine

4. Fake the assassination of a high-ranking military official

5. Point at Paul Newman and pull gibbon faces

6. Inadvertently quote *Roget's Thesaurus* in its entirety during an interview on *Entertainment Tonight*

7. Hold up a puppy and tickle its little bum-bum until it went pee-pee in his mouthy-hole

Grav grav gravity Jones
Tommy Lee Jones recently had his centre of gravity stolen. The thieves struck whilst Jones was playing a round of golf.

Moby Dicks
Tim Robbins and Susan Sarandon are to adopt a whale, after seeing a nature documentary. "Like hell it's gonna fit in the pool!" said an emotional Robbins.

Baby beware
Emma Bunton has been spotted almost walking under a ladder in Brighton. Shortly afterwards she could have been crushed by a passing bus, but wasn't.

Print(er)s uncharming
Steven Spielberg recently imprisoned a printer in a windowless room after the hapless inksman made a series of typographical errors on Spielberg's business cards. "Destroy all printers," Spielberg is alleged to have instructed a robotic friend.

Dwarfy saddle pops
Sebastian Coe recently took a group of midgets for a ride on a Shetland pony. "I only hope they feel normal for a short time," said Woody Harrelson, who was peering at the spectacle from inside a suit of armour dangling from a fucking tree or something.

Bubble and speak
Geri Halliwell is learning the Spanish for 'soap'. Once learned, she's hoping to speak it when next in Spain at shower time.

▲Hat depp-artment
Johnny Depp has spilt some liquid on his hat. It's not yet clear what the liquid is, but the word on the street says it's coffee.

◉ SPOTTED...

Claudia Schiffer in a photograph of a glamorous party also attended by **Harrison Ford, Kate Moss,** and **Jennifer Lopez**... **Jamie Oliver** advertising Sainsbury's supermarkets... **Ted Bellingham** on a packet of cheese and onion crisps... **Robbie Williams** gracing the front of this magazine... **Sean Connery** in a late-night showing of The Untouchables on BBC 1... **Michael Douglas** and **Catherine Zeta Jones** in the postcard rack of a Brighton movie memorabilia emporium... **Charles Dickens** on a ten pound note... **You** reading this sentence yes these words these words the ones you're looking at right now...

8. Deny the existence of Spain
9. Reverse the polarity of the Earth
10. Leap on Elton John's shoulders and demand to be flown to the nearest stargate

SOURCE: AFFLECKOPHACT.COM

News&that

LA Coincidental

EARSNATCHING UP THE HOLLYWOOD POWER HOLES

Actor **James Woods** has finally launched his own chain of themed restaurants. The first Planet Woods diner has just opened in Los Angeles, and features **James** himself strolling around and mingling with patrons, showing scant respect for authority and pretending to punch children. The next branch, due to open in New York in July, will feature a robot double of **Woods** kicking a milkman to death on top of one of the tables.

● Hot up-and-comer **Studs Martin** may play the villain in *Rat's Ass! The Movie*, but in real life he's proven he has a heart of gold. **Martin** was recently spotted taking some disabled children on a fishing trip. 'The kids had a really great time,' he said. 'Some of their wheelchairs got a bit stuck in the mud, but we all bonded when I killed a trout with a big rock. Then we shoved a stick through its head and roasted it over a fire until its eyes turned white and popped.'

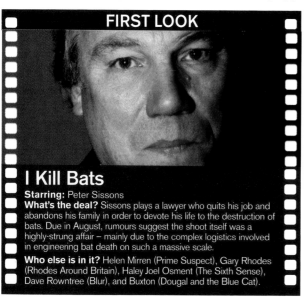

Clockwise from top left: James Woods gets too close to the camera; Dan 'Ghostbusters' Aykroyd wearing a shit cap; universally adored musician Phil Collins looking a bit John Reginald Christie.

● **Dan Aykroyd** recently announced plans to get his middle name legally changed to 'Ghostbusters' to ensure he will always be referred to as **Dan 'Ghostbusters' Aykroyd** in print. The trend seems to have gripped Hollywood by the glans: **Aykroyd's** move comes hot on the heels of **Pierce 'Dante's Peak' Brosnan**, and **Jamie 'Halloween' Lee 'Trading Places' Curtis** both making similar decisions.

● The most eagerly awaited blockbuster of the summer is *Sussudio*, a high-tech thriller based on the song by **Phil Collins**. Set during the late 1980s, the movie stars **Ewan McGregor** as the hapless **Collins**. Producers have promised the flick will feature a scene in which he does a little dance on a kitchen counter.

FIRST LOOK

I Kill Bats

Starring: Peter Sissons
What's the deal? Sissons plays a lawyer who quits his job and abandons his family in order to devote his life to the destruction of bats. Due in August, rumours suggest the shoot itself was a highly-strung affair – mainly due to the complex logistics involved in engineering bat death on such a massive scale.

Who else is in it? Helen Mirren (Prime Suspect), Gary Rhodes (Rhodes Around Britain), Haley Joel Osment (The Sixth Sense), Dave Rowntree (Blur), and Buxton (Dougal and the Blue Cat).

FACE OF THE WEEK

Karl Pouch

Who? The former face of hydrogen-flavoured breakfast cereal Funny Air Chomp, Pouch has turned his back on commercials and struck Hollywood gold.

Current buzz: Pouch has just started shooting *Nothing To Luge*, an extreme sports-themed action thriller in which he plays a small-time gambler ordered by the Mafia to ride a street luge through downtown New York with a petri dish filled with anthrax spores balanced precariously on his forehead. Russell Crowe co-stars as a disenchanted police sergeant who must clear the traffic blocking Pouch's way – or face the lethal consequences.

EXCLUSIVE!

Chaz Panther's
Controversial Video

Scorch takes a look at the shocking video everybody's talking about.

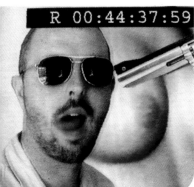

POP WILDMAN CHAZ PANTHER HAS an undisputed reputation for shocking fans with his videos – in *Bend Like the Night* he was digitally inserted into footage of the Jonestown Massacre dressed as a jester, and in *Triple A* he played a blind transvestite pope. But for new track *Drink My Genius* he's really pulled out all the stops – and found himself on the receiving end of the censors. MTV Europe is planning to only broadcast the controversial promo after 9pm, while US telly bosses are refusing to show it at all. *Scorch* got hold of an advance copy, and can confirm its content will leave even Panther's most hardened fans stunned and amazed and reeling around their living rooms like Norman Wisdom pretending to be lost in a hotel corridor.

The video opens with Panther brandishing a semi-automatic rifle, taking random pot-shots at terrified passers-by. Incredibly, these scenes were filmed for real in a suburb of St Petersburg. Three people were hospitalised for gunshot wounds and one elderly lady died. A clown on a motorbike then kicks the singer into a busy road, where seventeen cars run over his head in close-up as he delivers the chorus – a gob-smacking effect made possible by state-of-the-art digital imaging technology (the moment when one of his eyes pops out of the socket and bursts beneath the tread of an oncoming tyre cost an estimated $700,000 to create, and sets a new standard for ocular rupture simulation). We watch as Panther's brains dribble out of his skull and are pecked up and swallowed by a jackdaw. The rest of the video appears to take place inside the bird's mind – a fractured sequence of nightmarish images in which Panther:

● Paints the word INFANTICIDE on a school bus using a brush dipped in sick
● Glues a fox to a snowboard and hurls it into a turbine engine
● Applies for planning permission to demolish a Grade III listed windmill
● Ignores the "open other end" instruction on a packet of Jaffa Cakes
● Defecates on a photograph of the entire population of the world.

Director and prick Richard Smoghole Tenderfoot claims he didn't intend to shock. "We knew it might shake a few people up," he told us in an exclusive telephone interview, "but at the end of the day, it's just an artistic statement. That's all. We never set out to be controversial. The thought never even crossed our minds."

Tenderfoot is also at pains to point out just how unfazed he is by the ban.

"So the networks dropped a bomb on us. What's their problem? It's only a video! Well screw 'em. They can ban it to the moon and back if they like. They're always jerking artists around. Those pussies wouldn't know a work of art if it fuckin' flew through their window and stuck its masterpiece dick up their ass.

"These guys, they're like 'we're not playing your promo', and I'm like 'hey, I don't fuckin' *care*, mister'. It's their problem. They can sit and spin. *Sit and spin.* I'm really not concerned in the slightest. Like I keep sayin'. I just don't care. The guys at MTV, ABC, Fox, whatever… I've written to every *single one* of those fuckers, just to fill them in on how little of a nutshit I really give.

"I mean, really: sorry to return to the subject and all, but hey, you know: big deal. Big dicking deal. Like I give a squatting one. They can blow their goddam network out their frickin' TV ass. Whatever, y'know?"

Big dicking deal? The dawn of a new office catchphrase for the good people of *Scorch* towers, we reckon...

***Drink My Genius** is released at the end of the month.* ■

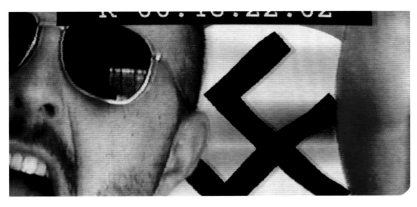

Why the st★rs are so fabulous
AND YOU ARE MUNDANE

Stars! On the face of it, they're just the same as you – they've got arms and legs, necks and faces, clothes and shoes. But the reality is quite different. You and the stars are actually poles apart, and always will be. To help you comprehend why, we've compiled the following handy guide...

ROBBIE WILLIAMS: Star

KURT COBAIN: Dead, but still better than you

★ The stars' sex lives consist of uninterrupted bliss. They regularly enjoy investigating every intimate millimetre of sexual partners 200 times more attractive than anyone you will ever so much as shake hands with.

★ Interesting things happen to the stars on a daily basis, turning them into more interesting people as a result – you simply become more tedious and bitter each day!

★ Stars hang around with exciting people. Think about your friends for a moment: if you combined all their character traits and life histories into a single person, would they be even half as exciting as Robbie Williams? No. In all honesty: no.

★ Even the most minor stars are rich beyond your wildest dreams.

★ The stars are surrounded by people who hang on their every word. Compare this to your life for a moment.

★ The stars have plenty of leisure time in which to exercise and keep fit. You slump at a desk all day, slowly blobbing yourself into a state of flabby despair.

★ The rich and famous are too busy to read magazines like this. Simply by looking at these words, you are underlining your limitless inferiority to the stars.

★ The stars' homes are filled with expensive designer furniture. If you borrowed a single chair from a celebrity, not only would it look ludicrously out of place in your house, but you'd have to walk around it on tip-toe, treating it gingerly because it was the "special chair". Simply put, you wouldn't be able to appreciate or enjoy it, because it would be out of your league. A celebrity would consider such behaviour insane.

★ An ill star can pay for treatment in the kind of top-flight private hospital that wouldn't admit you in a hundred million years, even if you were writhing in agony on the pavement outside with a shard of glass jutting out of your eye.

★ The stars are the only human beings to have fulfilled mankind's potential you and your kind are at the very bottom of the heap. Th is scientific fact.

★ Stars never sit down to dinner and resent the perso opposite them.

★ Stars don't need to cut out coupons from magazine before they can afford a sli of chain-restaurant pizza.

★ When stars want a glas of wine they go down to the cellar and open a fifty-year-old bottle. You have to take ferry to France just to save four quid on stuff they wouldn't even shit in.

★ When a star is snapped frolicking on a beach they look like a million dollars. In every single one of your holiday snaps you look like fat sack of crap.

★ When you go to bed at night you dream you're a star. No star has ever dreamed that they're you.

★ The stars' lives are an endless golden stream of

TED BELLINGHAM and MINNIE DRIVER: You'd love to be them

arties and laughter. Your fe consists of donkey ork, arguments and ubstandard sex.

★ The stars aren't always appy. But even at their most iserable, they're at least six mes more content than you ill ever be.

★ Stars don't spend their ves slumped on a sofa urling Doritos down their roat, gawping at a box splaying the antics of eople luckier, prettier, wittier, nd richer than themselves.

★ The stars are household ames. If you got up now nd knocked on your next-oor neighbour's door, they ouldn't recognise you.

★ Members of your own mily care more about what at Deeley is wearing than hether you live or die.

★ This magazine is devoted stars. There are no agazines devoted to you, nless someone's launched *hit Non-Entity Illustrated* nce we went to press.

★ Any male star is at least vo billion times more likely sleep with one of estiny's Child than an rdinary man is.

★ Stars are always ccompanied by a bouncer ho keeps them out of ouble. Anyone in the world ould just walk up and hurt ou whenever they felt like it.

★ Stars get invited to movie emieres in the West End. ou hire the DVD when it omes out. Which is better? atching a movie on a gantic screen in the ompany of several hundred the most glamorous people

in the world, or watching *Bridget Jones's Diary* in pin-sharp digital lonervision?

★ A star would never live in a house as shit as yours.

★ Stars don't need to set the video for *Holby City* and *Emmerdale* – they're in them. Between takes they laugh at the scripts and sneer about plebs like you.

★ Stars have a certain special quality you will never possess. You are so average you may as well be a smudge on a bathroom tile.

★ People wait for days in sleeping bags outside television studios and airports just to meet stars. They won't even pick up a phone to speak to you.

★ Stars never have to queue. They look down on those who do. You queue. You queue to meet stars.

★ Cynics point out that, just like you, the stars are human beings who have to go to the toilet. This is true. But unlike you, they could afford to pay someone to eat their turds and lick their bumholes clean if they wanted to.

★ Your partner would leave you for a star without a moment's hesitation.

★ In an online auction you, your children, and the entire contents of your house would be worth less put together than just one of Jennifer Lopez's pubic hairs.

SARAH JESSICA PARKER: Thinner, prettier, wealthier version of you

STEVE MARTIN: Not as funny these days; still ten thousand times funnier than you

MADONNA: Better than you

Celebrity Hang-out

What have kite done for me lately?

Janet Jackson glanced at a kite this week. The kite was being flown in a Los Angeles park as Janet's limo rolled past. It was a red kite.

Blonde ambition

Caprice is tipped to star in *Bum Bum Hat Castle*, a puerile medieval comedy written by an anonymous 14-year-old boy. She will play a dairymaid who giggles at a duck guffing into a bucket.

Dance yourself dizzy

White Mischief's Charles Dance turned heads in a London art gallery last week – literally. The *Passage to India* star was cranking a handle that made wax skulls revolve on a turntable, as part of an avant-garde installation by po-faced artbonce Sheb Penkington.

Segal's wheel outburst

Hollywood hard man Steven Segal has been fuming about wheels. "Okay, so they're round, so they take you places – big deal", he raged during a televised interview on WXBN7's *LA GabYak Tonite*. Segal's changed his tune since 1996 blockbuster *Under Siege* – in which he can clearly be seen standing next to a wheel, pointing and smiling for over fifteen minutes.

Thurrock Essex

If you want to rub shoulders with the world's biggest stars you'd be well advised to take a trip round the M25 and head straight for Thurrock. That's right, this month's Aspen isn't Antigua or Cannes - it's one of the shabbiest, dirtiest crap-holes on earth, shat by God beneath the shadow of the Dartford Bridge - and famous people love it. Brad Pitt, Elle Macpherson and Judith Hann are just some of the names spotted propping up the bar at the Moon Under Water, and it's worth checking out McDonald's just off Thurrock Way where our spies have reported seeing Russell Crowe, Samantha Mumba and Ray Stubbs kicking things near the bins and flicking milkshake at the staff.

THIS WEEK'S MUST-HAVE: Ideas

It-girl Victoria Hervey shocked party guests at the opening of new celeb hang-out Custards by turning up with nine ideas in her head. The blue-blooded heiress happily posed for photographers, and even let other recognisable people stroke the front of her mind, behind which the recently purchased thoughts were hiding. Victoria paid £600 for her ideas, but you can pick up nine similar creative inspirations for around £6 by reading a book or thinking about some things that you've recently seen or heard.

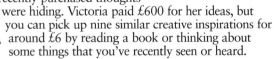

Wendy Westwood's Wild Wedding Walkabout

MUST HAVE PRICE £6

EEK! SECRET FEARS
What keeps the stars awake at night?

Bruce Willis – 'I'm terrified of being eaten by mice.'
Christina Aguilera – 'I sometimes get scared that I'll wake up and find a jockey in my hair.'
Matt Le Blanc – 'I have this dream where I'm operating Scooby Doo from inside his back leg. I'm pulling this lever to make him run, but no matter how hard I pull we can't get away from the ghost.'

Ted Bellingham Night TVGH 4 Saturday ★★★★

Ted Bellingham

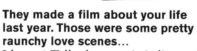

He's been the acceptable face of litter collection for over thirty years, and this week TVGH 4 throws a theme night in his honour. *Scorch* talks to Keep Britain Tidy figurehead **Ted Bellingham**.

You were born with tapered legs, one elbowless arm, no hands or feet, and a massive split in your back. Was it hard to get where you are today?
You forgot to mention that I don't have eyes or ears! [Laughs] But seriously, yes, it was extremely tough. With my disabilities I have to struggle just to stand up. That kind of background makes you a fighter. That's what's got me where I am. That and my passion for civic cleanliness.

You're on the side of countless cans, bottles, and crisp packets. Do people often recognise you in the street?
All the time, yeah.

What do they say?
Generally they just ask whether I'm really me, which is a bit strange at first! But you get used to it. Sometimes I get the odd one acting the smart-arse by asking where the nearest bin is, or trying to use my head as a Frisbee… but on the whole people are really nice.

They made a film about your life last year. Those were some pretty raunchy love scenes…
I know! Talk about artistic licence! They showed it going in and everything! I said to Minnie [Driver], "I don't recall my student days being quite so exciting…"

Ah, yes. You and Miss Driver have been the toast of the tabloids for some time now. Has the constant publicity put a strain on your marriage?
Fortunately Minnie and I are very, very much in love, so it's been relatively easy to cope with. Most of the time we find the stuff they write just really funny… there was this story in one of the tabloids recently where they said I was thinking of getting hair extensions. [Laughs] I mean, can you imagine that?

You'd look ridiculous
I know!

No, I mean really ridiculous. A joke. An absolute laughing stock. You look strange enough as it is. If I were you I think I'd kill myself.
Steady on.

We're about to run out of space so I'd just like to say that I was only joking just then. Actually I think you're brilliant. Everything you do is wonderful, and you have a beautiful wife. Congratulations!
Thanks, that's very kind.

Can I touch you?
No. I am not real.

Ted Bellingham Night is on TVGH 4, Saturday night.

All aboard the shitwit: buffoons sail the seven seas in *Ship of Fools*

Worthy Gawps

Ship of Fools
11.00pm TVGH 4

'Oooh ooh ooh oooh ooh – do we not sail on a ship of fools?' So sang Erasure on their 1988 top ten smash 'Ship of Fools'. But as Andy Bell stood on *Top of the Pops* miming those words while Vince Clark pretended to accompany him on a Roland synthesiser, could either man have envisaged a time several years later when many of the same television sets upon which members of the public were currently viewing them would be tuned instead to a popular documentary series with an identical name to their hit single?

It seems unlikely. And yet *Ship of Fools* is now one of the hottest shows on British television. The formula is simple – take a group of real-life fools, put them in control of a full-size ocean liner, then sit back and film the results. Already the public have been wowed by

collisions with tugs, a fatal mishap involving an anchor, and an utterly hilarious five-day argument in which the difference between port and starboard was debated by two people too stupid to even know the difference between up and down. Filming the series was the easy part, according to producer Shettlewin Gumbrace. The hard task was recruiting such a spectacularly stupid 'crew'. 'We placed adverts in the papers, but soon realised that the kind of extreme dimwits we wanted wouldn't be reading in the first place – and certainly couldn't get it together long enough to write an application and stick it in the post.

'Eventually we had to gather them together by going out into the streets with glove puppets on, and waving them around in the air and asking people to follow us if they wanted to have a go on a boaty-woat.'

So what's been his favourite moment so far? Gumbrace grins in a way that suggests it's an easy question. 'The episode where Tom got seasick, definitely,' he smirks. 'There he is, spewing away, and he's so frightened and confused by what's happening he starts trying to run away from his own sick while it's still flying out of his head.

'He ran the length of the deck, spraying vomit like a mobile fountain,' chuckles Gumbrace. 'Absolutely priceless.'
Katie Pierce

Big Look Circus
8.00pm TVGH 4

Ever wondered what those milky orbs in the front of your face are? Wonder no more: they're your eyes! And the makers of *Big Look Circus* are hoping you'll be using them to stare at their 24-hour voyeurific webfeed, as a member of the public agrees to undergo nine weeks of relentless surveillance. Woo hoo.
Marilyn Cramp

101 Amazing facts

46. During the Falklands War, the British army stitched television sets to sheep's backs so that soldiers crouched in bushes and trees for long periods of time could catch the occasional glimpse of a show.

47. Televisions of the future will have a special compartment to keep salad chilled.

48. In Turkey, it is traditional for bridegrooms to stay at home the night before their wedding and watch an episode of *The Lonely Owl*. The show is much like *Happy Days*, except the main character is an owl and instead of being set in 1950s Milwaukee, all the action takes place on the summit of a mountain of ice-cream.

WEDNESDAY

TV Terrestrial

 1

 2

 3

TV GH 4

9.30am Daily Mail Island

Another edition of the astounding social experiment in which volunteers are stranded on a remote island without access to any form of media other than the *Daily Mail*.
Week 20. The castaways' language has almost entirely devolved into a baffling combination of rhetorical questions and arrogant snorts.
Producer Dee Stopian

10.30 Teletext Cinema

Hollywood blockbusters re-interpreted as static screen-by-screen storyboards constructed from ASCII text and giant blocks of colour, to the sound of an easy-listening soundtrack. This week: Brendan Fraser and Rachel Weisz star in *The Mummy*.
Producer Paul Rose   *Digitiser...480*

1.35pm Neighbours

Carl glues a small dog to the wall of his garage and spends the afternoon sitting in a deckchair while it forlornly cranes its neck in the direction of an out-of-reach Bonio nestling on a nearby bench.
Producer Dipshit Pickletwist *Oztitles...888*

2.05 Reverberation Bay

Australian soap set in a coastal beauty spot with a unique natural echo delay. Cindy bawls the news of her pregnancy to Scott as he stands by the water's edge – forgetting that three hours later the entire conversation will ripple across the bay in full earshot of ex-husband Paul.
Producer Robin Tandy   *Subtitles...888*

3.00 Condorman Fucks Up

Taking his dog for a walk, Condorman meets a spectacularly attractive woman with whom he immediately blows his chances by dropping his ice cream in her bra and clumsily attempting to stab it out with a knife, apologising and crying all the time.
Producer Log Nonymous   *Subtitles...888*

9.40am The Flintstones Movie – the Animated Series

Confusing animation based on the live-action film, in which the characters are drawn to resemble the actors in the movie and not the original cartoon.
Producer Har Nar   *Subtitles...888*

11.15 Tower Of Babel

Light-hearted quiz in which a panel of cosy Radio 4 regulars attempt to decipher sentences spoken by people with regional accents.
Producer Yo Bo   *Phonetic subtitles...888*

12.00pm Here Comes The Cash Cow

Caper movie starring **Bernard Cribbins** and **Lionel Jeffries** as two scheming layabouts who hatch a plot to steal a safe from the local butcher by smuggling their mother Joan into his stockroom disguised as a carcass of beef.
Eddie...............................Bernard Cribbins
Joe.................................Lionel Jeffries
Joan..................................Irene Handel
Butcher.....................Wilfred Hyde-White
DIrector Crikey Smithson (1964)

3.30 John Peel Narrates...

The Story of Coathangers. Britain's most popular DJ lends his distinctive voice to another low-key documentary.
Producer Mick Phallus   *Subtitles....888*

4.00 Parliament Behind Socks

The morning's events from the Commons recorded in longshot by a camera tethered to Westminster Bridge with two Argyle socks dangling in front of the lens.
Producer Simon Artdegree

6.25 Police, Camera, Impossible

High-speed car chases that defy the laws of physics and logic, created using utterly convincing state-of-the-art computer graphics. This week: police chase a double-decker bus around the rim of the Grand Canyon, and a stolen Ferrari driven by Marilyn Monroe hits an ice-cream van filled with golden bowling balls and flips over 15,000 times.
In digital widescreen with Dolby Surround and additional flashing colours for anyone with a set of fucking disco lights connected to their television.
Producer Alistair Stewart *Subtitles....888*

9.25am Jakki Shelf

'I Don't Understand The Instructions and Can't Find the Allen Key'.
Producer Ligament French *Subtitles...888*

10.30 The New Adventures of Burke and Hare

Animated series tracing the antics of Edinburgh's notorious body snatchers turned serial killers.
5. Wake up Burke! When Dr Knox calls at their house demanding more bodies for a medical lecture, Hare can't rouse Burke – who's been up all night practising strangling techniques.
Producer Gordon Man   *Subtitles...888*

12.00pm New Series Shop Gimp Theatre

New series in which ASDA and B&Q employees currently appearing in television commercials get the chance to re-enact classic dramas in their own distinctive manner.
1. The Browning Version.
Producer Talon Gent   *Subtitles...888*

1.35 Nurofen Bay

Eye-and-ear fucking Australian soap opera featuring a cast of sunburnt tattooed youngsters in clashing shirts and garish patterned trousers using loudhailers to screech tonguetwisters at one another on a fluorescent green set cluttered with revolving spirals and distortion mirrors, bathed in the subliminal flicker of a bright pink malfunctioning strobe.
Week 64. Lee interrupts Marie's accordion practice by turning up in a silverfoil suit and reeling around with a Catherine wheel on his head and a pair of metal keys strapped to his feet.
Producer Migraine Henly *Subtitles...888*

4.00 Wife In The Next Room

1. Darren shouts through the serving hatch that he would like to spend some time together in the lounge, and is struck by a bowl of spaghetti, which lands on him like a wig.
Producer Talon Walon *Subtitles...888*

10.00am Who Killed Kinnear?

Dramatic reconstruction of the investigation into the death of Roy Kinnear, who fell from a horse while filming *The Return of the Three Musketeers* in 1988. Features some of his showbiz friends as themselves, introducing hilarious slapstick clips from throughout Roy's career. Coroner Barry Cryer presides.
Producer Howe Unpleasant *Subtitles...888*

3.30pm Bullying Today

Tips and tricks from schoolyard tyrants across the nation, including a special report on taunting the overweight. Introduced by Ross Kemp.
Producer Mary Qunt   *Subtitles...888*

4.30 New Series Lifeboat Vet Cops

Return of the popular fly-on-the-wall documentary series chronicling life at the Penzance Veterinary Lifeboat Constabulary.
1. Lights Out. It's the height of August, but as crowds pour into Cornwall hoping for a glimpse of the solar eclipse, it's business as usual for the seabound police vets – breaking up an illegal dog fight on a fishing trawler and tending to the injured animals.
Did the lifeboat vet police come to the rescue of your pet? Have you slept with a vetcop? Do you think animals should be murdered at sea? The Kilroy team would like to speak to you: 070 170138
Producer Tossy Tosstoss *Subtitles...888*

5.00 Biggins – You Buird Lairway

Historic re-enactment of Japanese wartime atrocities, with Britain's most popular pantomime dame again at the sharp end. This week, yelping campily, Biggins declares himself physically unable to lay any more track through the Burmese jungle – so instead is made to dig a mysterious pit roughly six feet long at gunpoint.
Producer Bo Widdle   *Subtitles...888*

REGIONAL VARIATIONS

NEXT DOOR

6.00pm Sounds Like an Argument

6.15 Scraping Furniture

7.30 That Was Definitely a Thump

9.00 Shouting

10.45 Eerie Silence

LONDON

7.30pm London is the Greatest

8.10 Hooray for London

10.00 London London London

11.30 London!

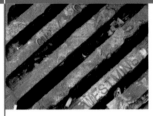

8.30pm Back on the beat: the spineless detective with his ear to the ground

8.30pm Jellyback

Detective series starring Robson Green. Born without a spine, Detective Adam 'Jellyback' McKinnon has conquered prejudice and disability to become the police force's leading expert in carpet-level crime. 3. *Bending Over Backwards*. McKinnon goes undercover to solve the murder of a famous limbo-dancer.

Were you born without a spine? Do people gasp in astonishment as you somehow use your feet to drag yourself along the pavement while remaining flat on your back? Does your head ricochet painfully off each step whenever you descend a flight of stairs? Do you watch friends doing sit-ups with a combination of envy and impotent rage? Do people stop you in the street to ask if you'd like to borrow a couple of vertebrae, then stroll away laughing? If we asked you about it on television, is there any chance you could burst into tears for us? How about if we rubbed a piece of fucking onion into your eye? What then, you little shit? Our research team would like to speak to you: Call now on 020 7656 7018
Producer Jessica Length   Subtitles.....888

9.30 Mick Hucknall's Pink Pancakes

Mick entertains visitors to Brighton Aquarium with his unique brand of crazy scrotal capers.
Producer Minnie Stootighttomention   Subtitled...534

10.00 Ezekiel's Clockwork Quim

Continuing the musical dramatisation of the true story of Victorian inventor Ezekiel Rodican-Brown and his attempts to perfect the world's first fully-functioning brass vagina. 3. *Quim on the Loose*. Ezekiel's plans suffer a setback when an early piston-powered prototype chews through a wall and escapes, screwing everybody on the Balls Pond Road. Includes the songs *Stop That Cunt!*, *Testing My Contraption*, and *Clit Like a Rivet*.

10.30 High Low Culture

A Scottish post-graduate laying in a hammock argues that *The Brittas Empire* was better than Hamlet.
Producer: Desmond Skinny

12.00am The Ten Tasks of One-Armed, One-Legged Hercules

7. *Changing a duvet cover in the back of a moving caravan.*
Producer Pam Ampersand   Subtitles...888

1.00 Switch Me Off or They Will Eat You

Four hours of eerie faces and ghostly noises specifically designed to scare any children who might be watching on a portable set in their bedroom.
Producer Bo Geeman   Subtitles.....888

7.40pm Boo bloody hoo: grim movie drama that's half as cheerful as this

7.40pm Harrowing Drama of the Year

Mark Kermode introduces three finalists from the competition that honours the most gritty and uncompromising British films of the year. Following the screenings, dedicated phone lines will accept your votes in each of the following categories: *Best Picture, Best Actor, Best Actress, Most Provocative Sequence, Harshest Language, Murkiest Lighting* and *Lengthiest, Most Unbearably Fucking Tedious Slow Bit*.

7.50 With This Ring

Hard-hitting tale of grinding poverty and domestic violence starring Ray Winstone as an embittered and impoverished ex-boxer trapped in a loveless marriage to his own daughter.
Dave Hammond...RAY WINSTONE
Tessa Hammond...TILDA SWINTON
Zammo..LEE MACDONALD
Director Gary Oldman (2001, 18)   Subtitles...888

10.10 You Are Here

The lives of four teenagers on a Glasgow housing estate intertwine in a web of meaningless despair and blank-eyed defecation.
Danny..................................MICHAEL TIMOTHY-EVANS
Harpo..............................LEONARD FFOLKES-ROYSTON
Moose...CHARLES BEDFORD
Jabba...............................HRH SIMON GREGORY-PITTS
Clueless Social Worker.....................CAROLINE CATZ
Director Tim Roth (2001, 18)   Subtitles...888

12.55am Welcome to the Shitbox

Depressed by gambling debts and the recent death of his estranged wife, an unemployed electrician penetrates a dog in a graveyard and is jailed for gross indecency. Having struck up a relationship with the prison psychologist, he is on the verge of putting his life back together when, in one of the most unpalatable sequences ever committed to celluloid, a malicious prison guard spikes his breakfast with LSD and bashes his head against the floor six hundred and ninety three times in a row before pissing on his back and ramming a chairleg up his arse. Music by Chris Rea.
Mick English.......................................RAY WINSTONE
Sarah Millington...............................CAROLINE CATZ
Guard...PIERS HERNU
Director Tim Oldman (2001, 18)   Subtitles...888

2.30 Cunt

Nathan Barley reads an edition of *Sleazenation* magazine from cover to cover while smoking a joint in a Tokyo hotel room.
Producer Lo-Slung Denim   Subtitles...888

TV Terrestrial

3

1.05am Wow Ooh Boom: ultra-high quality sparkly shit for DVD bores

8.30pm Your Shout
Community programme. A member of the general public moans about a minor issue in a stilted and unconvincing manner. Should be called 'You're Shit' instead, really.
Producer Marianne Real   *Subtitles...888*

9.00 Fuck Your Felt Aunt
Psychotic gameshow hosted by Paul Ross. Two frustrated bachelors try to beat the clock in a contest to design and build life-sized effigies of their own aunts using offal for insides and coloured felt for skin. The maker of the most attractive 'Felt Aunt' wins a night with a top London prostitute, while the other is forced at gunpoint to drag their creation into the middle of the road and perform full sexual intercourse with it until both are crushed beneath the wheels of an oncoming car.
Producer Sigmund Freud   *Subtitles...888*

10.30 New Series
Scott Pocker C.E.O.
Ground-breaking action series funded by and starring Scott Pocker, the 38-year-old Chief Executive Officer of the Pocker Entertainment Group.
1. Beware the Angry Mindthieves. Wandering through a Seattle warehouse for a *Fortune* magazine cover shoot, Pocker stumbles across a gang of misguided protesters plotting to control the nation's youth with a collection of opinion-warping fanzines.
Producer Scott Pocker   *Subtitles....888*

11.30 The Metaphor Dimension
Heavy-handed allegorical sci-fi. *Domestic Bliss*. A balding, middle-aged husband is abducted and taken to a planet made of flabby bellies where his wife is being screwed by a young, athletic gardener.
Producer Darilis Crouse   *Subtitles...888*

1.05am Gawper's Paradise
Plotless sequence of audio-visual spectacles designed to mesmerise the imbecilic owners of top-of-the-range home entertainment systems.
2. Explosions. Massive detonations erupting in true 16:9 widescreen, with NICAM digital stereo and support for Dolby Surround and THX audio. Music by Huey Lewis and the News.
Do you have an incredibly expensive 'home cinema' system? Is it hooked up to a DVD player? Are you proud of the crystal-clear sound and immense 16:9 screen dominating the room? Do you watch films like Armageddon and Mission Impossible on it, and find yourself aroused by the relentless thud of the sound effects? Why? What's the point? Why don't you just fucking kill yourself? Our researcher would like to speak to you: call now on 020 7656 7018.
Producer Angela Laddergun   *Subtitles...888*

4

8.00pm The Eyes Have It: Relentless, despicable voyeurism and powerful jets of steaming ammonia in *Big Look Circus*

8.00pm New Series
Big Look Circus
Fascinating televisual experiment that tests the boundaries of voyeurism. Starting tonight, a member of the public has volunteered to spend nine weeks strapped to an operating table beneath an immense glass eye and an undulating latex phallus. The eye broadcasts uninterrupted facial close-ups while thousands of internet users visit the official website to repeatedly click an icon that makes the penis spill a fat stream of hot piss directly into the participant's left retina.
Are you prepared to have your every waking moment subjected to the scrutiny of the British public? Can we stick a camera down your pants and sort of wiggle it around? Or maybe push the lens right up against your anus, then administer a drug that causes flatulence, so we can film the sphincter flexing as you pass wind and screen the results on a gigantic electronic hoarding overlooking Piccadilly Circus? Perhaps you'd like us to engineer an ordeal in which a pig in a Stan Laurel mask gives you a protracted browndicking while we use the global satellite network to beam your squirms of discomfort to millions of ugly gawping shits worldwide? It's okay, we'll pay you. The Big Look Circus team would like to speak to you: call now on 0207 00004
Producer Goggle K. Sickwatch   *Subtitles...888*

9.30 Indiana Jones and the Doomed Office Romance
2. When Karen asks Dr Jones to help her correct an inexplicable formatting error in a Microsoft Word document, the erstwhile archaeologist responds in a slightly over-eager fashion, fixing the problem with unnecessary bonhomie before offering to help her with any future technical queries at the drop of a hat.
Producer Diddlewop Jiggleknot   *Subtitles...888*

11.00 Ship of Fools
Hilarious documentary series in which a crew of backward imbeciles is left in charge of a full-size ocean liner set adrift in the Mediterranean – with hundreds of hidden cameras onboard to capture the action as a real-life comedy of errors is played out.
2. Check Out Captain Dumbo. Leonard inadvertently causes disaster when, frightened by a seagull, he veers the ship directly into the path of an oncoming speedboat.
Producer Tarrant Sneer   *Subtitles...888*

12.30pm Condorman Fucks Up
When Andrew O'Hagan accidentally drops his fork on the floor at a sophisticated literary luncheon, fellow guest Condorman launches into a protracted comic impersonation of a mentally handicapped man, loudly slapping the back of his head and moaning 'duhrrr, by nabe's Andrew' for a full five minutes, until the air of silent hostility emanating from the remaining diners starts to detract from his performance.
Producer Jesus Cripes   *Subtitles...888*

DIGITAL, SATELLITE AND CABLE

DISTURBED CHILD NETWORK

9.00am Teddy in the Dock
This week, Teddy is found guilty and sentenced once again to be tortured all day long.

10.00 FILM: Three Ninjas Start Crying

11.45 Stare At Your Sister
Uncomfortable game show.

12.15pm 101 Great Finger Painting Headfucks
45: A picture of daddy lying down dead.

1.30 The All-New Talking Breadknife Show

2.30 FILM: Chitty Chitty Bang Bang Bang Bang Bang Bang Bang Bang Bang Bang Bang
Classic children's favourite inexplicably interspersed with contemporary footage of gunfire.

4.25 FILM: Rugrats in Hospital

6.05 Blackout

INFINITY PLUS ONE

10.15am Big Wheel of Fortune

10.45 Ultra-Bill

11.15 Time Team Forever

1.30pm Emmerdale Plus Plus

2.00 Quickly Quickly Changing Rooms... *Quickly! Quicker Than That!*

2.30 Megaphone Jackanory

3.00 Ready, Steady, Cook, Cook, *COOK*

3.40 FILM: Paint Everybody's Wagon

5.10 Dallas and EastEnders at the Same Time

6.00 FILM: 10,001 Gigantic Dalmatians

7.50 Jo Brand Filmed Through a Magnifying Lens Shouting Putdowns at a Man with a Penis Two Atoms Long

8.00 FILM: Carry On Shawshank Redemption Up The Towering Inferno

10.20 Late Review
With three Mark Lawsons and sixteen Tom Paulins.

WISPY HORRORBOX

The toothless horror entertainment channel.

11.15am The Zany Werewolf

12.30pm Frankenstein's Bus

4.55 Zombie Croquet

5.45 FILM: The Creature From the Nice Lagoon

7.25 Stephen King's Spooky Limericks

10.00 Scooby Doo

11.30 FILM: The House That Dripped a Substance Which Looked Exactly Like Blood But Turned Out To Be Water With Rust In It

1.15am Face at the Window! Oh, it's Dave

BRUNEI-SULTAN 1

7.00am Good Morning Your Majesty

8.00 Your Favourite Hotels

10.00 We Salute You

11.30 Bill Gates – Pah

1.30pm We Salute You

2.40 Brunei: The Glory Years

3.40 Asia's Most Powerful and Legitimate Monarch

6.50 We Salute You

9.30 You and Your Cars

11.30 National Anthem

CORNERSHOP

The local shopping network.

8.25am Newspaper Zone

10.00 Anyone for Cigarettes?

11.25 Lottery Ticket Time
Dimwits queue up for a slice of the impossible dream.

12.30pm Furtive Porn Mag Purchaser's Happy Hour
No female assistants – guaranteed.

1.30 Three Double Deckers for the Price of One

2.00 LARGE CHEST for Sale

2.30 Phonecards and Stamps

3.45 Greetings Card Plus
45. Happy Retirement.

4.00 Schoolkid Mayhem Zone
Maximum two viewers at any one time, please.

5.30 More Cigs; Closedown

CHRISTMAS ETERNAL

The channel where every day is Christmas Day.

6.00am Wake Up and Scream Like a Demented Bloody Banshee
Christmas morning mix of cartoons and live entertainment for early-rising youngsters and depressed insomniac loners, hosted by Michaela Strachan and Brian Sewell.

7.15 Santa Spits On Sinners
US animation.

8.40 S Club 7's Nativity Block Jam
The fresh-faced pop group tell the story of the birth of Christ in their own toe-tapping style. Includes the songs *Three Wise Guys And One Cool Kid* and *Saviour at the Decks*.

9.15 A Very Thundercats Christmas

10.45 Chucklevision
Britain's most wizened and suspect comedy duo help out in Santa's toy factory. Contains tiresome havoc.

12.30pm Sissons Greetings
A very special yuletide celebration broadcast live from the home of stern-faced newsreader Peter Sissons. Guests Nicholas Witchell and Moira Stuart play Pass the Parcel while Peter stands awkwardly in a corner silently grinding his teeth. Includes hourly news bulletins.

2.30 EastEnders
Characteristically uplifting seasonal edition of the popular soap opera. Having fallen off the wagon, Phil wakes up next to the body of a murdered prostitute – but is he really to blame? Dot is still hearing voices, while Mick staggers bleeding into an alleyway to discover a foetus being eaten by a wolf.

4.30 Cliff's Inexplicably Morbid Yuletide Singsong
The 'Peter Pan of Pop' performs a series of abnormally gloomy seasonal ballads, including *Christ Died Horribly, Feasting on a Turkey's Corpse, Simon the Boxing Day Arsonist* and *Fuck Christmas To Hell*.

7.15 Film: Santa's *Sunny Delight* TM Adventure
Comic yuletide caper starring Henry Winkler. It's Christmas Eve, and Santa Claus is delivering presents as usual – until he stumbles across a sinister plot to steal the world's supply of his favourite fruit juice lookalike. With the help of a resourceful group of children of various racial origins, he must resort to violent slapstick and thwart the thieves before the unthinkable happens and the secret magic recipe for fresh-tasting, lip-smacking, nutritious *Sunny Delight*TM – the great taste kids go for – is lost forever.

Santa Claus..........................HENRY WINKLER
Head Terrorist.............................ART MALIK
Short Sidekick.............................JOE PESCI
Jimmy.................................NELSON GRINNER
Jenny........................TINKERBELL DEADEYES
Yum-Yum Good..................LING-SOO YOUNG
Willis Homeboy...................GARY COLEMAN
Princess Sunny D...REECE WITHERSPOON
Director Sayles Pitch

9.00 Yuletide Telly Blinkers
Meaningless spiral shapes provide something to stare at, plus a convenient excuse not to talk to visiting relatives.

11.00 A Very Dubya Christmas, Y'all
Chilling live broadcast in which the American President demonstrates his status as the world's most dangerous man by holding his index finger one milimetre above the nuclear button and staring at it fixedly for four solid, silent hours.

3.00am FILM: Death Wish You a Merry Christmas
Violent thriller starring Charles Bronson. Mild-mannered architect Paul Kersey has his cosy existence torn apart when regressive hypnotherapy reveals repressed memories of a harrowing childhood incident involving an aroused department store Santa. Vowing revenge, he tours the seedy in-store grottos of New York armed with a sharpened screwdriver and a brick...

Paul Kersey...................CHARLES BRONSON
Chico...BASIL EZZAT
Loco....................................LOU ANGUIZAMO
Dead Santa......................CHARLES NAPIER
Dead Santa..........................STACY KEACH
Dead Santa............................HENRY WILLS
Dead Santa.........................WILLIAM KATT
Aghast Child...................RICKY SCHRODER
Director Michael Winner (1980, X)

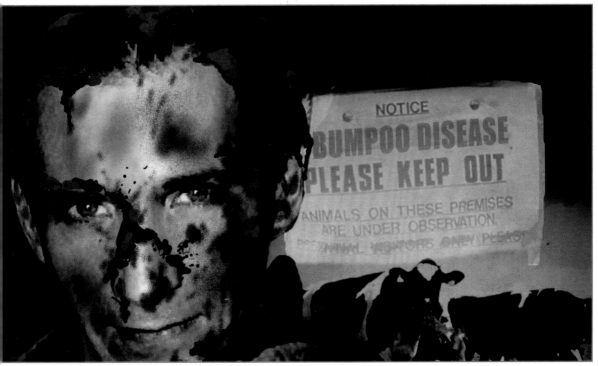

Brown and out: the moo-moos done a plop-plop again in *Return to Widdleplop Farm*

MOVIE CHOICE

6.00pm Last Play
Carry On Mounting Dead Animals

Saucy comedy starring **Sid James**. Struggling taxidermist Sidney Ramsbottom tries to boost sales by spraying his motionless menagerie with a powerful aphrodisiac.

Sidney Ramsbottom.................SID JAMES
Molly Ramsbottom....................JOAN SIMS
Sir Royston Fingerwolf...KENNETH WILLIAMS
Bert Cowpoke........BERNARD BRESSLAW
Sally Eelsquat..........BARBARA WINDSOR
Tarquin Stoatfucker..CHARLES HAWTREY
Dr Jizzingalloverapigsback........JIM DALE
Director Stout Yeoman (1972, PG)

7.35 Biafra Va-Va-Voom

Another outing for this Elvis classic with the young rocker cast as singing rally driver Chet Slick. With the world rally series due to reach a climax in famine-era Biafra, Slick suspects jealous race mechanic Lopez of messing with his car – and messing with his girl. Includes the songs *Revin' for Adventure, Civil War Hotsie,* and *Starting Grid Malnutrition Blues.*

Chet Slick.............................ELVIS PRESLEY
Lopez...DAVID NIVEN
Marie...GINA FANTASIE
Director Bizz Welcome (1966, U)

9.30 Indiana Jones and the Local Council

All-action blockbuster starring **Harrison Ford** and **Jennifer Lopez**. Tiring of a life of non-stop adventure, Dr Indiana Jones retires to a picturesque cottage in Hampshire. All is peaceful until the local paper uncovers plans to allow a gypsy encampment to settle just outside the village. Donning his trademark fedora, Indy forms an unlikely alliance with the glamorous head of the local chamber of commerce, and together they embark on the quest of a lifetime – eventually leading to a nail-biting showdown in a local magistrate's court.

Dr Indiana Jones.............HARRISON FORD
Miriam Salter.................JENNIFER LOPEZ
Council Official..............CHARLES NAPIER
Local Newsagent........ROBBIE COLTRANE
Director Nimby Pissant (1995, PG)

11.10 Conan the Bumbanger

Puerile action film starring Arnold Schwarzenegger as a mythical homosexual warrior.

Conan..........ARNOLD SCHWARZENEGGER
Writhing Victim.............................JUDE LAW
Director Ryan Ham (1987, 15)

12.45am Return to Widdleplop Farm

Big budget sequel to *Widdleplop Farm* starring **Ralph Fiennes**. When farmer Harold Walsh arrives at his new Tuscan small-holding with his beautiful bride Millie, it seems he has put the excremental horrors of the last six months behind him – until one morning while digging for fresh coriander he strikes deep into Italy's main sewer, sending a geyser of molten effluence thousands of feet into the sky, where it destroys an airliner carrying 257 obese diarrhoea sufferers to a specialist hospital in Madrid, who rain down around Walsh like water balloons, bursting on impact and showering him and his wife with guts, shit, and adipose tissue while a fountain of urine and faeces continues to spew from the ruptured Earth below, launching arc upon arc of puke, tampons, and piss-sodden stools into their faces and down their throats as they gasp for air like frightened drowning children, clawing and panting through foul-smelling plumes of opaque steam and methane gas, as dense and overwhelming as sulphurous volcanic fog spluttering from the clenched and angry red-raw ringpiece of Hell's backside itself.
Director Peter Jackson (1999, 12) *Subtitles..888*

49. The world's angriest TV dentist is Norway's Pal Groest, whose hit show *I Kick Your Mouth Out* regularly commands an audience of 8m viewers.

50. A man in Gateshead, Tyne and Wear, has been casting suspicious glances at his television for fifteen years in the mistaken belief it once tried to steal his shoes.

51. A leading Japanese electronics manufacturer is understood to have developed 'the ninth button', which will be common to all sets by the year 2016. When activated, the ninth button makes all programmes 'more modern'.

How we used to watch...

TV Schedules from the *TV Go Home* archives

1984

1977

7.00pm Like Father, Like Sambo
Searing social comment and cheap racial jibes combine as a working-class bigot discovers the black next-door neighbour currently dating his daughter is also his own long-lost son.
Producer Keith Badteeth

7.30 Department of Anarchy
Documentary series that pokes its eyeholes behind the scenes of the Government's new Department of Anarchy, established to address the needs of the nation's punk rockers. 1. The think-tank team approves designs for a new national flag consisting of a fluorescent photo-collage of the Queen in a tartan binliner. Raymond hurls a chair through the window and Julie spits at some men.
Producer K-Y Jelly

8.30 Wolverhampton Tinselpants
Glam-pop music show live from Wolverhampton's Wulfrun Centre. Featuring music from Spag Bol, Alroight?, Diamond Cider and the Space Invaders, The Cooters, and Denim Truckway. Plus dancing from the Robin Askwith Glitterchops Ten and an exclusive live performance from David Bowie's new band Faggy Moondust and the Crystal Beekeepers.
Producer Royston Hoist

9.00 Lib Up, Fatty
Sitcom. An overweight feminist from Balham plots to overthrow men, but finds herself continually thwarted by a randy radio Disc Jockey with whom she is forced to share baths in order to conserve energy.
Producer Dick Stubb

5.50pm TV Job Centre
The nation's last three remaining jobs advertised on-screen for ten minutes.
To apply for the job at the bakery, phone 01 702 2002
To apply for the job at the care home, phone 01 702 2003
To apply for the job kicking miners to death, phone 01 702 2004
Producer Yosser Hughes
Subtitles...888

6.00 Aspen
Glamorous US soap depicting the absurdly opulent lives of Colorado's richest dynasty, the Prosperos. Tammy-Lou catches Jim bathing in asses' milk with his aerobics instructor. Barney ends up in a coma when his gold locomotive collides with a carriage full of industrial-sized shoulderpads on its way to TC's designer warehouse.
Producer Aaaaaaaron Clockjock Jnr, III
Subtitles...888

6.30 How You Will Die
Terrifying eighteen-week long demonstration of precisely what will happen to your body when the nuclear bomb drops. Episode 10 – Six seconds after impact. Your eyes boil in their sockets before popping like champagne corks and dribbling down your chargrilled cheeks. Meanwhile, it's not looking good for your shrapnel-blasted abdomen.
Producer Jenni Quatro
Subtitles...888

7.00 Designer News
Jan Leeming sits in a pastel pink wire-and-neon studio introducing footage of strikes, sieges and riots.
Producer Alma Geddon
Subtitles...888

7.15 Noel's Chuckle Castle
Gunge, pranks, dancing, and close-ups of Shane Richie going cross-eyed. Michael Ryan undertakes the Whirly Wheel challenge and some tinsel lands on Noel's head.
Producer Michael Lobb
Subtitles...888

7.55 Video Whizzcast
Amazing hi-tech fun as an engineer demonstrates just some of the special effects capabilities of the Quantel paintbox by making footage of David Copperfield slide around the screen, fold itself into a cube, and then spin out of view. Music by Thomas Dolby and Special A.K.A.
Producer Thatcher Buggles
Subtitles...888

8.15 20 GOTO 10
Home computing show. Michael Rodd discovers how to generate random numbers on his Commodore, while Todd Carty explores the world of 'high-resolution graphics'. Plus a peek behind the scenes at the making of William Tang's 'Horace Goes Skiing'.
Producer Sinclair Tandy
Subtitles...888

9.15 FILM: Mollycoddle High
Five mismatched US teens are forced to share a nuclear bunker during a false alarm and discover they have more in common than they ever imagined, as they struggle together to overcome minor psychological problems endemic of their unbelievably spoilt existence. Music by John Parr and Sly Fox.
Kooky Alice...ALLY SHEEDY
Jessica Shutquim..............................MOLLY RINGWALD
Jack Jock...EMILIO ESTEVEZ
Smiling Non-Threatening Cool Guy.......ANDREW McCARTHY
Principal Tightass...............................CHARLES NAPIER
(Director John Hughes, 1984, Certificate 'A')
Subtitles...888

101
Amazing television facts

52. One crazy fan of the show *Airwolf* has a television shaped like a wolf, which he keeps suspended in the air with twine.

53. The first recorded British television-related death occurred in 1983, when a man was smothered to death in a branch of Rumbelows by an unsecured 28" Trinitron.

54. The smallest working television ever made was a wrist-TV for ants built by Sony technicians in 1995 to celebrate the election of an ant to the Japanese Parliament.

55. In Italy, it is against the law to play the part of a female prostitute if you are considered by ex-boyfriends to be shit in bed.

56. In order to broadcast pictures to houses on the tops of hills, transmitters have to bowl the signal underarm at an upward angle of 48 degrees.

57. Television is great.

58. In 1992, ITV received a record number of complaints over a suggestive scene in *Heartbeat* involving a badger and a man in a sack.

59. If a snail glides across a television screen, it becomes positively charged with ions capable of magnetically attracting leaves.

60. The Vatican has its own TV channel, which broadcasts pictures of the Pope accompanied by accordion music, plus re-runs of *Ever Decreasing Circles*.

61. The first occurrence of swearing on British television occurred in 1971 during the infamous sitcom *It's Grim Up Fucking North*.

62. 98% of university students said they'd be prepared to push a splintered chairleg up their arse in order to land a job presenting a prime-time television show.

63. Televisions of the future will require the viewer to coax out the programmes with ice cream and some kind words.

64. The most popular Belgian Quiz show is called *I Is Piss Right*.

65. If you stare through the window of an electrical store at a bank of TVs you will become obsessed with spotting an image of yourself. Unless you are an actor or sports star, it's unlikely you'll be on any of the screens; this is when you begin to search for your reflection in the shop window; and this is when children begin to think of you as a weirdo and call you names like Rabbit Man.

66. In order to fit an entire television into your mouth, you'd have to first remove your skull and reinforce your facial muscles with special leather straps.

67. French televisions have a hole at the back for viewers to shit into.

68. One of the worst broadcasting gaffes in history occurred on the 7th of May 1978, when an Australian continuity announcer accidentally swallowed his own brain while trying to pronounce the name 'Lieutenant Uhuru' during an introduction to an episode of *Star Trek*.

69. Before television controllers introduced the concept of schedules, programmes were live and would run until the actors got bored, fell asleep or ran out of plot. In 1937, an unknown actor Will Cinders managed to drag out a dying scene for 42 days, writhing alone on the deck of a ship, clawing at his eyes and crying.

70. Scientists at Glasgow University have invented a device that allows deaf people to know when the balls in a televised game of snooker have collided with a satisfying 'clack' sound, by sending an electrical pulse through their torsos and making their livers vibrate.

71. The zaniest American used-car-dealer's commercial of all time was shot in 1976, and depicted salesman Jay 'Hooray' O'Shea in a giant foam cowboy hat, riding a kangaroo around on the hood of a speeding Oldsmobile, squawking through a loudhailer shaped like a duck's bill. In an unrelated incident, O'Shea was later convicted of child molestation, causing the clip to be replayed rather awkwardly in the middle of sombre local news reports.

Apocalypse Wow: Tragedy brought to life as never before in *The Vietnam War in 3D*

Worthy Gawps

The Vietnam War In 3D
11.00pm TVGH 3

They say the first casualty of war is truth – but actually it's picture quality.

Despite carnage on a scale never seen before, World War I is virtually unwatchable, with the Battle of the Somme, in which the male population of whole towns were wiped out in a single morning, reduced to grubby smudges that make a mockery of modern home entertainment systems.

WW2 is similarly fuzzy. It seems incredible now, but D-Day forces landed in front of handheld monochrome cameras. It wasn't until Spielberg's widescreen *Saving Private Ryan* recreated the devastation on those beaches that the conflict became truly entertaining.

Even the more recent Gulf War was characterised by murky night vision, and it wasn't until Kosovo that full stereo was used in reports, earning it the epithet of 'the first Nicam War'.

Most Vietnam footage is of similarly poor quality. But the discovery of this incredible footage by a stereoscopic movie unit means that we can now enjoy the Tet Offensive, Agent Orange and the Mai Lai massacre in blisteringly pin-sharp 3D.

You almost feel like that little girl is running terrified through your living room. Great stuff.

Dave Hilton

Hilltop Brasshead Bergerac
10.30pm TVGH 1

When *Bergerac* star John Nettles hung up his badge from the *Bureau des Etranger*, he found himself in a wasteland.

'I'd go to castings,' recalls Nettles, squatting on the porch of his Cheshire bungalow, 'and all people would say is "He's the guy from Jersey" or "I only see him as a Channel Islands policeman", or "Ooh-hoo, hark at the prick from *Bergerac*."

'It was only after I'd got the job as a detective on *Midsommer Murders* – a role quite unlike that of Bergerac – that I could stand to hear his name again.'

Then came *Hilltop Brasshead Bergerac*, the idea of fellow Jersey star Charlie Hungerford, actor Terence Alexander.

'I still keep in touch with Terry because he has a fitness cycle that I like to use occasionally,' reveals Nettles, carefully studying the flight-path of a goose with a set of binoculars.

'The old scripts are fantastic,' laughs Nettles, taking another long sip of cream soda, 'There's one where an old friend of Charlie's is actually a hitman who's come to the island to bump off a crafty local businessman.

'And you know, it almost works better being performed by a gigantic brass head than it did back in Jersey.'

Mitchell Coolwatch

TV GH 1

9.00am Daily Mail Island
Another edition of the astounding social experiment in which volunteers are left stranded on a remote island without access to any form of media other than the *Daily Mail*. *Week 21*. The pilot of a light aircraft crash-lands on the beach and is offered food and shelter in exchange for twenty years of uninterrupted slavery.
Producer Dee Stopian   Subtitles...888

10.00 Skyclimber 2000
Action series starring Lee Majors as Aspen detective John Kable, who patrols the alpine skies in an experimental police cable car, slowly fighting crime on symmetrically opposed mountains.
3. Ski You Next Tuesday. Kable glides to the top of Mount Legworn to investigate allegations of cheating at a ski lodge beauty pageant, but his inquiry is short-lived when he spots a distress flare fired from a neighbouring peak...
Producer Runcible Spoon Subtitles...888

11.35 Tom and Jerry
Tom momentarily squints and grows a Fu Manchu moustache when an orchestral cymbal vaguely representing a traditional oriental hat crashes onto his head, before the aftermath of a minor explosion leaves Jerry with dark skin, bulging eyes and fat, red lips, to the accompaniment of a sarcastic refrain of 'The Camptown Races'.
Producer Hal Hopefoot   Subtitles...888

2.45pm Dot to Dot News
Current affairs with Peter Sissons, accompanied by an uncompleted join-the-dots puzzle in the top right corner of the screen for apathetic viewers with wipe-clean markers.
Producer Alma Geddon Subtitles...888

4.00 The Ten Tasks of One-Armed, One-Legged Hercules
8. Crossing a rope bridge wearing a big bowler hat made of lead.
Producer Jinks Casey   Subtitles...888

TV GH 2

9.00am Moo Moo I'm a Cow
Unconvincing children's series based on the rarely-challenged notion that animals can tell you what they are, in English, after making their characteristic noise twice.
Producer Yip Sherwood   Subtitles...888

9.30 That's My Boy
More morgue fun as corpses are wheeled around on trollies while their loved ones try to identify them, carrying buckets of coloured water.
Producer Anne Baby   Subtitles...888

10.40 My Friend Billy
Epilogue. Having lost a large portion of his penis during the rake attack, Billy takes precautions to ensure his still substantial phallus no longer resembles a snake – while the girl next door, shaken by guilt and disgust, starts cutting herself...
Producer Log Nonymous   Subtitles...888

1.55pm New Series DVD Easter Eggs For Terrestrial Scum
1. Storyboards for The Abyss
Producer Reb Buy   Subtitles....888

3.30 Willow vs Sprats
Live scientific experiment to determine the relative durability of a full-grown willow tree and a plastic bag full of live sprats, by striking the tree repeatedly with the sprats until either the fish burst or the tree falls over.
Producer Damon Blue   Subtitles...888

4.55 Ainsley's Last Suppers
More deathbed cuisine as Ainsley Harriott continues his tour of Britain's hospices. This week, a terminally ill watchmaker from Norwich enjoys a Mediterranean feast.
Producer Trent Jackson   Subtitles...888

6.10 Fuck 'Em, They're Foreign
Footage of overseas disasters accompanied by comedy music and sound effects.
Producer Chris Peatissue Subtitles...888

TV GH 3

9.25am Jakki Shelf
'I Thought I Dumped Your Body in the Lake'.
Producer Ligament French   Subtitles...888

12.00pm On the Sacrificial Buses
Dark pagan remake of the popular sexist comedy. Stan and Jack journey to the remote Scottish community of Summerisle to watch Blakey meet a gruesome end inside a gigantic wicker man.
Producer Lord Summerisle Subtitles...888

3.00 Hooky!
Comedy series following the adventures of Lucy Bedford, whose hands were replaced by hooks following an accident in a poorly-maintained gardening centre.
2. You Can't Make an Omelette... Lucy decides to help out in the kitchen of her father's restaurant.
Producer Stephen D. Wright
Subtitles...888

3.30 Strapped to Your Dad
Troublesome teenagers strapped arm, leg and hip to their fathers in order to feel his erection rousing against them as he is shown wild pornography over their shoulder.
Producer Donkey Portillo   Subtitles...888

4.00 And the Band Played On – the Animated Series
US children's cartoon series based on Randy Shilt's best-selling history of AIDS and HIV in the early 80s. *Episode 5*. Dr Francis attempts to have San Francisco's gay bath-houses closed down, while Dr Gallo is near to understanding the behaviour of the T-cells in infected patients.
Playsets featuring characters and locations in this series are on sale at outlets of the World Health Organisation.
Producer Hereton Laneplop Subtitles...888

4.40 Divorcee News
Up-to-the-minute current affairs geared toward the faintly embittered.
Producer Alma Geddon   Subtitles...888

TV GH 4

9.15am Soho Olympics
All the action from this year's London media olympics, introduced by Steve Rider.

9.30 Transient Dodging
Rich media professionals avoiding, ignoring, and snubbing the homeless, live from the heart of Soho Square.

11.10 Clueless Pavement Scooting Dimwit of the Nanosecond

1.05pm Futile Age Denial
Increasingly saggy and decrepit males in their thirties parade from the doorways of production houses dressed in clothes that make anyone other than a thin youngster look like a fat neurotic clown.

2.55 Runner Molestation
Harrowing office toilet action as ugly coke-fuelled series editors jab nicotine-stained fingers into the crotches of confused and impressionable 19-year-old runners reeling from an evening filled with hollow compliments, promotion offers and massively spiked drinks.

3.50 Oblique Reception Area Lifestyle Magazine Flipping
Job applicants sit in the slickly characterless lobbies of independent production companies thumbing through copies of *Dazed and Confused*, awaiting interviews with mercenary shark-eyed cunts.
All times subject to change if drug tests overrun, which they inevitably will.
Producer Sal Godswipe   Subtitles...888

4.00 Whispersome Companion Cinema
New series showcasing classic movies with annoying comments whispered over the top, as if delivered by a companion in the cinema, in order to slightly spoil it.
1. Live And Let Die in the company of an elderly female relative repeatedly asking which one is James Bond.
Next week: a physics student constantly pointing out precisely why David Cronenberg's The Fly doesn't make sense.
Producer Hamlet Tease   Subtitles...888

REGIONAL VARIATIONS

PETER SISSONS' HOUSE

6.00pm News

6.15 News

7.30 More News, Read in a Very Stern Voice

9.00 Classic News: 1973

11.15 ADULT FILM: Autocue Nights

3.5" FLOPPY

6.15pm report.doc

7.00 my_photo.jpg

8.15 Abort, Retry or Cancel?

9.00 Quick Format

11.35pm Ha ha! HA HA HA! Hilarious blue language that'll make you burst your guts

7.30pm A Question of Close-Ups of Amateur Teen Fucking

Pornographic gameshow from the makers of *A Question of Sport*.

Producer Selwyn Clickathon   Subtitles......888

8.00 Bored Diner News

Read by a man idly picking wax from a restaurant table candle while his fiancée stares at her napkin.

Producer Alma Geddon   Subtitles...888

9.00 Ezekiel's Clockwork Quim

Continuing the musical dramatisation of the true story of Victorian inventor Ezekiel Rodican-Brown and his attempts to perfect the world's first fully-functioning brass vagina.
4. By Royal Appointment. As word of his invention spreads, Ezekiel is summoned to Buckingham Palace to demonstrate his device to Prince Albert – but Queen Victoria appears distinctly unamused. Includes the songs *Quim for a King, Push It In There Your Majesty, Sunk to the Regal Nuts,* and *Arise Sir Cuntmaker.*

Producer Tickle Fortheringay   Subtitles...888

10.30 Hilltop Brasshead Bergerac

Challenging new series in which John Nettles lurks inside a gigantic mechanical model of his own head made from brass and Victorian rivets, manipulating facial expressions via a bewildering system of cranks and pulleys in order to re-enact key scenes from old episodes of Bergerac, conversing when necessary with another mechanical head representing Charlie Hungerford situated on a neighbouring hill.

Producer Poodleflip Disco   Subtitles...888

11.35 Pottymouth Chucklescreen

Rib-tickling high-tech interactive fun for viewers who find bad language funny in its own right. Simply select a swearword from the list below, hit the corresponding button on your keypad, and enjoy an entire side-splitting hour of the word emblazoned boldly and hilariously across the centre of your television screen.
To see the word PISS, press 1.
To see the word SHIT, press 2.
To see the word FUCK, press 3.
To see the word CUNT, press 4.
To see the word CUNT in big letters, press 5.
To see the words BUM BUM PISS CUNT flashing on and off in an absolutely immense font while someone repeatedly reads it out loud to the delight of an applauding studio audience, press 6.

Producer Delete Insert-Home   Subtitles...888

12.00am No way out: paranoid whisperings to drip ice on your sorry bones

8.00pm Cunt

In bed, high on six Vodka Red Bulls and a pint of Staropramen, Nathan Barley penetrates an equally drunken female acquaintance, and following thirty-seven strokes of mounting enthusiasm finds himself begging out loud for permission to ejaculate on his lover's face – an act which, despite her inability to decide, he carries out regardless moments later, unleashing a gross eruption of gummy translucent plasm all over her cheeks and hair shortly before regaining his breath to gaze down at the startlingly memorable sexual image he has created, marred only slightly by the faint sound of sobbing.
Are you an undeserving London media do-nothing poshboy who's just fired an incredible torrent of selfish grey semen across the face of a sexual partner? Did you spend the evening telling her lies and feeding her drinks in nigh-on psychotic pursuit of your grimy little tryst, caring not in the slightest for her thoughts or cares or conversation, enraptured instead by the prospect of sliding your grasping, mollycoddled hands all over her body? What dark sexual predictions fluttered through your superficial mind as you sat on the edge of the bed sliding off your brand-name trainers, sewn together in South East Asia by a half-dead young mother pumped full of amphetamines by a sweatshop boss intent on fulfilling a last-minute order within 48 hours? And as a mighty manmade storm lashed the window, and the TV behind you spat dead Palestinians across your naked back as you sowed your dim narcissistic seed, did you feel a thin apocalyptic tendril gently coiling itself around the central pillar of your mind? You didn't, did you? But you should have. Yes, you REALLY FUCKING SHOULD. FUCK you HATEFUL Barley CUNTHEADS. Fucking FUCK YOU FUCKING ALL. Our research team would like to speak to you: call now on 020 7656 7018

Producer Lo-Slung Denim   Subtitles...888

11.00 Hip Hip Hooray for the Dangletramp Ball

Outrageous series in which poor people from around the country are strung up like marionettes and made to dance to Bontempi organ covers of Eighties soft rock hits for the entertainment of a marquee full of guffawing upper-class youths reclining on huge settees, slurping champagne from the hollowed-out skulls of council estate children, and periodically staggering outside to hurl bricks at a tramp swinging grotesquely back and forth from a set of 'high-society' gallows caked in gold and diamonds.

Producer Peregrine Mansion   Subtitles..888

12.00am Nil Escape From Dreadtalk Planet

Chilling programme in which insomniacs across the nation mutter their darkest late-night fears into the telephone and have their accumulated whisperings broadcast live, accompanied by as-it-happens NASA footage of Earth slowly turning, starkly alone in the nonsensical blackness.

Producer Shishkabob Plankton   Subtitles...888

3

11.00pm Gee whizz: try to duck all the fucking guts flying out of the screen

8.00pm Doogie Howser's Million Dollar Tinfish Blast Zone

Spectacular three-hour special broadcast live from a disused industrial sector in Detroit in which former child star Neil Patrick Harris stands within a large chalk circle guarding a novelty clockwork fishing game from would-be anglers armed with fishing rods and magnets. Each fish caught is worth a million dollars, and members of the public are welcome to enter the fray – but Harris is equipped with two handguns, a semi-automatic shotgun, four large boxes of high-explosive grenades, a crowbar and a whip, and has been granted the authority to use deadly force against anyone within a 100m radius by the Mayor of Detroit, provided he retains one foot inside the chalk circle at all times. Music by Badfinger.
ADDITIONAL RULES: Anyone prepared to be gunned down by Neil Patrick Harris may enter the contest at any time. Each fish is worth $1,000,000. Rods may be no longer than three metres. The use of firearms and cloaking devices will result in immediate disqualification. Electromagnetic equipment generating a field greater than 200 milligauss will not be permitted. All entrants should wear conical hats fashioned from chicken wire and tinsel; those without headgear will be treated with open indifference by an attractive researcher. Doogie Howser's Million Dollar Tinfish Blast Zone is a co-production from WBMG Detroit, The Violence Channel and Zeppotron.
Producer Scroll Lock Pausebreak   *Subtitles...888*

11.00 The Vietnam War in 3D

Six years in the making, this haunting documentary makes powerful use of previously unseen stereoscopic footage shot by pioneering amateur cameramen to bring the tragic conflict to life in ways more mind-blowingly awesome than ever before.
Contains flying intestinal tracts and digitally remastered explosions in Dolby Surround. No glasses? Call 0908 757474 to order yours now!
Producer Charlie Incoming   *Subtitles...888*

11.30 The Metaphor Dimension

Allegorical sci-fi. *Just Desserts*. A bad-tempered boss is captured by aliens and displayed in an intergalactic zoo beneath a sign reading 'Bad Tempered Bossus'.
Producer Bob Sterling   *Subtitles...888*

12.00am Wife in the Next Room

Darren tries to reach through the serving hatch with a stick, hoping to draw his wife into hugging distance, but accidentally scratches her face with the hook and is soaked by an amazing jet of blood that pins him against the wall as his wife screams and screams and screams.
Producer Flap Dangle   *Subtitles...888*

4

7.00pm World party: cynical shots of exotic faces that help shift units

7.00pm Cynical Multinational Global Ethnic Diversity Shitvert of the Year

Rock 'n' Roll CEO Scott Pocker introduces the awards ceremony that seeks to reward the creators of the year's most omnipresent 'global carnival' commercials for hazily sinister transatlantic technology firms. Categories up for grabs include *Best Use of Gap-Toothed Chinese Peasant, Most Hopeful Glance Heavenward, Blandest Mission Statement, Best Delivery of Corporate Catchphrase by Angelic Caucasian Toddler, Flashiest Edit, Largest Conceptual Schism Between Faceless Product and Contrived Mardi Gras Atmosphere, Briefest Glimpse of Black Businessman, Sequence Most Unsettlingly Reminiscent Of That Bit In Soylent Green Where The Old Man Is Shown Footage Of The Natural World In All Its Glory Shortly Before He Gets Killed And Turned Into a Flavourless Protein Snack* and *Richest Cunt in the Room*.
Contains footage of objectionable Dave Stewart lookalikes bounding eagerly onstage to collect awards while trying to appear too cool to care.
Producer Tom Paternoster   *Subtitles...888*

9.00 CGI Extrapolation Moviehouse

Continuing series in which a short piece of existing footage is fed into the latest in Computer Generated Imaging systems and extrapolated into a two-hour motion picture.
2. The 30-second Cinzano ad in which Leonard Rossiter pours a drink on Joan Collins is transformed into a full-length romantic comedy.
Next week: that advert where an animated fox tries to persuade a polar bear to get off a Glacier mint is elongated into a family musical.
Producer Ken Ufeelit   *Subtitles...888*

9.30 Soul Man Now

Documentary profiling the life and career of Mark Watson, a white man who fifteen years ago blacked up in order to win a college scholarship and the girl of his dreams. Today, Mark, still blacking up, is the pastor in a thriving Alabama Evangelist church, a close confidate of Jesse Jackson and a leading member of the NAACP.
Producer C Thomas Howell   *Subtitles...888*

11.00 Indiana Jones and the Doomed Office Romance

4. When Lando Calrissian, Former Baron administrator of the Cloud City of Bespin, takes a job in the Swinton office and immediately begins using his rogueish charm to great effect on Karen, Dr Indiana Jones slumps behind his monitor, grumpily rearranging his desktop icons.
Producer Diddlewop Jiggleknot   *Subtitles...888*

DIGITAL, SATELLITE AND CABLE

TV SATELLITE

YELLOWING PUNCH NETWORK
New channel based on old copies of *Punch* magazine.

7.00am Cartoon
Bearded Man on a Very Small Desert Island with One Palm Tree Discovers a Message in a Bottle He Himself Sent Several Years Ago.

8.00 Alan Coren
What Life Would Be Like if I Really Did Have Eyes in the Back of My Head.

10.00 Cartoon
A Man and a Woman Sit in Front of a TV and Pass Comment on the Blandness of Their Lives.

10.30 Hunter Davies
Why I Like Bradford.

12.00pm Victorian Cartoon
Old Man in Armchair, in Some Distress at Seeing Younger Woman Not Wearing the Correct Dress Hem Length For April in the Oxford And Cambridge Club, While Being Eyed by Foreign Gentleman Who Has a Suggestive Manner.

6.00 News From Cricklewood
With Alan Coren.

TENUOUS EROTICA PLUS
All very vaguely erotic programming, all the time.

9.00pm Several Chickens On a Rotisserie
With huge yawning orifices.

10.00 Young Woman Stroking a Pear

11.00 Steeplejack At Work
Blowing up a large steeple.

12.00am A Live Salmon Flapping On A Fishmonger's Counter

1.00 The Dome Of St Paul's Cathedral

1.30 Dough Rising

2.00 A Wriggling Pot Of Live Maggots

3.00 Wet Leather Chaps

4.00 Wobbly Red Jelly Topped With a Cherry and Some Dribbles Of Cream

5.00-7.00 Dead Pig 24

U-CHOOSE CINEMA
Interactive pay-per-view digital movie channel which offers the viewer complete control over every element of a multiplex-style blockbuster, thereby guaranteeing satisfaction. Today's options (use keypad to select):

1: Location New York / Rio / Venus / Morecambe

2: Male Star Cruise / Cage / Costner / Van Der Beek

3: Female Star Bullock / Kidman / Roberts / Emberg

4: Genre Thriller / Comedy / Romance / Lame Titilation

5: Title
Deadline / Countdown / Get Down / Go Down / Wahey!

6: First Line
'Your honour' / 'Jesus!' / 'Morning Stan' / 'Oof'

7: Last Line
'Because crime don't pay' / 'That's what I call a man of the people!' / 'Fancy blowing the saviour of the world?'

8: Baddie
Renegade Government agents / Arabs / Monster / Kevin Bacon / Unconvincing psychopath

9: Tag Line
'Time to kick ass!' / 'Time to kick ass again!' / 'Time to kick everybody's ass!' / 'Contains gunfire and titties'.

10: Sequel Number
II / 3 / The Return / Final

11: Theme Tune Huey Lewis And The News / Teddy Prendergast / Limp Bizkit / The Indigo Girls / Stockhausen

12: Cameos Donald Trump / Bette Midler / Ted Bellingham / Aerosmith / Selwyn-Gummer

13: Period Contemporary / 70s / 2035 AD / Barbarian Times

14: Level Of Male Nudity
No nudity / Chest / Butt cheeks

15: Level of Female Nudity
No nudity / Chest / Is this film French or something?

BASIC TV
10 PRINT "I AM SKILL"
20 GOTO 10

RETIRED ANIMATED ADVERTISING STAR BUSINESS NEWS
6.00am Business Breakfast
With Buzby and the Griffin.

9.00 Asia Round-up
Reaction to final prices as the markets close in the Far East with Tufty the RoSPA Squirrel.

10.00 Market Watch
With Money and Access in London and the Cadbury's Caramel Rabbit in New York.

1.00am Fiscal Lunchtime
Round-up of the breaking business trends and prices with the tortoise from those Creature Comforts adverts.

2.00 New Business And Financial Market Round-Up Afternoon Watch
As-it-happens money-oriented news, forecasts, analysis, round-ups, speculation and comment with the dancing skeleton from the Scotch videotapes commercial.

5.00 Closing Prices Market Round-Up And Watch
The closing prices, plus up-to-the-moment analysis, in-depth speculation, backward-looking foreplanning and chatter with the Lurpak Butter man.

9.00-6.00am Money Watch Round-Up Nightly
Rolling and rotating business news, comment, analysis, hypotheses, speculation, revelation and charts with the Muller Rice Captain.

TXT MSG TV
3.00pm Antqs Rdshw
3.30 Only Fls + Hrss
4.00 Inspctr Mrs
5.00 FLM: N / NW
6.30 Hv I Gt Nws Fr Y
7.00 1 Ft > Grv
7.30 Cn St
8.00 *s > Thr iiiii
8.30 FLM: 4 Few $ +
10.00 Nws@10
10.30 Who Wt 2B £1m?
11.30 FLM: Fri 13 Pt 2

THE CIDER CHANNEL
6.00am Strongbow News
7.00 Bulmer's Daily
11.00 The Scrumpy Jack Hour
12.00pm Why I Like Cider
Johnny Vaughan.

1.30 Woodpecker's World

4.00 A Very Merrydown Afternoon

6.00 Cyder or Cider: The Big Spelling Debate

6.30 FILM: The Cider House Rules

8.30 The Second World War In Cider
Historical documentary. With the Sixth Army surrounded at Stalingrad, and Germany cities facing a devastating barrage of bombs day and night, Hitler ponders having a nice glass of Shloer.

9.00 Cider, Cider, Cider, Cider, Cider, Clder, Cider, Cider
Heavily cider-themed show.

10.00 Ci-der! CI-Der! CI-DER!
Programme for the deaf.

10.30 I Love Gaymer's Old English
Nostalgia.

11.00 K
Strong Cider.

12.00am Perry – It's Cider, But Made With Pears Instead Of Apples
Re-run documentary.

12.45 White Lightning Now

1.00 Diamond White Nights
Adult entertainment.

1.30 Dry Blackthorn 24

DAD NETWORK
6.00pm War
7.00 Old Snooker
7.30 A Bit of a Cowboy Film
8.00 News In Medium Depth
8.30 Sports Cars
9.00 Nice Konnie Huq
9.30 Charlie's Garden Army In Slow-Motion
10.00 Some 70s Football
10.30 Dire Straits Live
11.00 Lingerie Update
11.30 ADULT FILM: What That Boy Might Be Doing With Your Daughter Upstairs

Blonde ambition: Peter Sissons takes the lead in *The Denise Van Outen Story*

MOVIE CHOICE

6.00pm Songs of Praise: The Movie

Big-screen version of the long-running Sunday evening religious programme aimed at the soon-to-be dead. A crazed lunatic has planted a nuclear device somewhere in Chichester, and Thora Hird must race around the city introducing hymns and smiling at filmed inserts of interviews with local craftsmen if she is to find clues to the bomb's location.

Thora Hird..HERSELF
Armin Dugong..................DENNIS HOPPER
Canterbury Jones............STEVE BUSCEMI
Esther McVey.....................DARYL HANNAH
Monotone Silversmith...BRUCE CAMPBELL
Director: Sam Raimi (1992, 15)

8.20 Say You, Say Me

Existential drama based on the popular song of the same name, starring **Lionel Richie**. Having recounted an awesome dream in which people in the park are playing games in the dark, a musician delivers a heartfelt plea for universal solidarity.

Lionel Richie..........................LIONEL RICHIE
Director Lionel Richie (1984, PG)

9.50 The Denise Van Outen Story

Woefully miscast biopic starring **Peter Sissons** as breast-obsessed blonde personality Denise Van Outen. As her relationship with bebop irritant Jay Kay draws to a close, the former *Big Breakfast* superstar reflects on the incidents that shaped her life...

Denise Van Outen............PETER SISSONS
Jay Kay..................................MARTIN CLUNES
Johnny Vaughan.................CHRIS PATTEN
Liza Tarbuck....................MOIRA STEWART
Vanessa Feltz..........................TONY HAWKS
Kelly Brook............................BRIAN SEWELL
Chris Evans.....AN UNFOLDED DECKCHAIR
Julian Clary................MIGHTY JOE YOUNG
Bob Geldof............................FRED BASSET
Director Thomas Jizzlobber (2001, 15)

11.10 Tough as Fuck

Blockbuster action movie conceived and written by a panel of hormone-addled 14-year-old boys. Unconventionally violent police sergeant John Fuck finds himself on the trail of a ruthless gang of nude female criminals who unwind between heists by jumping around on a trampoline.

John Fuck......................BRIAN BOSWORTH
Foxxi Titshower.........PAMELA ANDERSON
Director Kurtis Zits (2000, 15)

12.45am Film Premiere Bare-Assed Hen Cocktail at Gunpoint

Fascinatingly brutal cinematic experiment in which **Tom Cruise, Elisabeth Shue** and the rest of the cast of the lightweight 1988 romantic drama *Cocktail* are forced at gunpoint to re-enact the entire film shot-for-shot – but this time dressed head-to-toe in gigantic hen costumes with the bums cut out.

Brian Flanagan Hen...............TOM CRUISE
Doug Coughlin Hen..........BRYAN BROWN
Jordan Mooney Hen.....ELISABETH SHUE
Kerry Coughlin Hen..............KELLY LYNCH
Coral Hen.............................GINA GERSHON
Director Vince Motherfucker (2001, 15)

2.15 Adults Only The Faker

Star-studded sexual horror. Disappointed by the poor quality of Internet celebrity fake nudes, a deranged surgeon begins decapitating famous female stars and sewing their heads onto the naked bodies of pornographic models at unconvincing angles.

Dr Philip Craven..................JEREMY IRONS
Angela Craven......................GUDRUN URE
Gillian Anderson................................HERSELF
Sarah Michelle Gellar...................HERSELF
Jeri Ryan......................................HERSELF
Sergeant Mcintyre......CRAIG FERGUSON
Director: David Cronenberg (2000, 18)

101 Amazing facts

75. If you un-spooled all the videotape used to record the world's TV soaps, bundled it all together and dropped it from a helicopter circling above London, police estimate that at least 98 car thieves would get tangled in the mess.

76. Dieticians claim eating undercooked mince whilst watching television is good for the digestive system. This is because the sight of mild entertainment causes a warm vapour to be released from the rear of the viewer's eyeball, re-cooking the ingested meat.

77. Dutch scientists have developed a television set powered by the viewer's own sense of self-loathing.

81

The food kids *love*

GRIMY FACTORY

Dead Hoof-and-Eyelid
Meatlike Grill

NOW conforms to food safety guidelines

Semi-prime mashed-up cow corpse patties with additional skin flakes and chips of shattered thighbone

450g net weight

Well, the kids on council

estates love it anyway - because they're stupid. Look at them, the imbeciles. Hovering expectantly round the table, mouths agape like whales homing in on an undulating shoal of plankton.

Ugh. Hideous, greedy, selfish little dimwits. They probably think food grows on trees. And in some cases they're right. But that's really not the point.

Give them something

to bung their guts up for six minutes – like our new Hoof-and-Eyelid Meatlike Grills.

We take only the mangiest cattle and herd them into trucks at knifepoint. A masked swordsman slices the good bits off while the cow's still breathing: what's left is prodded toward the intake hatch of a gigantic machine, which beats, strips, and purees it into mulch.

This slop is moulded int

a vague steak-like shape, frozen, tossed inside a brightly coloured box, and carted to a supermarket. And that's where you come in, wit your money and your kids and you broken fucking dreams.

So go on. Gobble up a Meatlike Grill while our CEO sits at home dining on pheasant.

It's all you scum deserve.

GRIM FACTORY

now**biter**

LATEST EDITION £20.00

OX-KICKING / CHILLUM HOLSTERS / INVISIBLE MENTAL CINEMA / FASHION
LUB SILENCE / JASON THORKWELL / PHOTO-TEN-PHOTO / NEW IBSEN 9Z-10
HE LEOPARD FROM LIME STREET / EXTINCTION SEX NOW / FLUURRRRGGHH

The ONLY lifestyle guide that respects YOU as much as YOU respect IT.

EDITOR: NATHAN BARLEY

nowbiter
FEEDBACK

Hanging around

At last someone's had the fucking nerve to write about arranged suicides (**nowbiter** #2). This is a problem that is on the up (619 arranged suicide deaths in the UK alone last year) yet the government refuses to take a stand. I'm from Nottingham where arranged suicide is very much considered a rite of passage. On my thirteenth birthday my parents gave me a digital watch and a certificate telling me that I would hang myself in the kitchen on the eve of my fifteenth birthday. I ran away that day and I'm still hiding. My best mate Marcus wasn't so lucky; last Christmas he cut his legs off below the knees and bled to death, just as his parents had arranged. People need to open their eyes to what's going on, respect for removing the blinkers. Loved the piece on Lady Christ.
Stevo, via e-mail.

Vex-istential angst

By criticising Damo Slurpunk (**nowbiter** #2) you are, as he predicted, retransintellectualizing. Just remember, that for all her fucking ideas, Simone de Beauvoir used to regularly chomp on Sartre's cock as he kicked her around the streets of Paris.
Lucac Freed, Germany

Stink bombed

Great then-skool Whizzer and Chips / Whoopee shoot (Fleetway of the Warrior, **nowbiter** # 2) but you forgot to mention where you can buy the Pongo Snodgrass jodhpurs. Must have! Must have!
Isobel Abbington, via e-mail

Sorry. We're not interested in those any more and couldn't be bothered to look it up.

Northern Uproar

So "MC Theocritus" (Letters, **nowbiter** #2) thinks the Northern patio scene is a non-starter? Perhaps if he stopped sneering at everything outside the M25 for ten minutes, he'd have time to actually come up here to Bradford and see for himself just how alive it is. There's a whole world going on outside the London-centric world you Soho-whores inhabit, as I'll show you all when I move to the capital following my sociology degree. Over and out, motherfuckers.

Dan Fottingham-Klent, Bradford

daydream BELIEVER

Clifford Pazzorilli writes screenplays in his head. No cast, no film crew. Just his own thoughts, projected on a screen in his mind's eye.

"I've envisaged epics you couldn't comprehend," he explains over coffee and a roll-up at the Bluebird café, as he unwinds for ten minutes during a hectic Wednesday afternoon shopping expedition on the King's Road.

The 27-year-old hit upon the idea after a short film made during his student years got a frosty reception at its premiere. "The audience couldn't handle it," he shrugs. "The ones who didn't walk out stood up and hurled shoes at the screen. I knew then I must be doing something right."

"Not long afterwards, it dawned on me – since making a film is such a personal experience, why not keep it entirely personal?"

Over the last eight years Pazzorilli has imagined a range of movies so diverse, it would turn most writers pea green with envy. Most star himself. This year alone he's already appeared in an ironic action thriller – think Die Hard scripted by John Lennon – and an "unashamed erotic fantasy" in which he sleeps with an attractive next-door neighbour. All inside his head.

"She's a real person – she lives in my street. I saw her walk past my window and instantly cast her in the lead."

"The beauty of it is she doesn't even know," he says with a cheeky twinkle.

His next project will take him into unchartered territory. "I'm thinking of tackling a Western. I'm interested in taking established genres and completely turning them on their head; re-inventing them in a totally original way. It's a journey. It's a quest."

But the Western will have to wait. For now Pazzorilli contents himself with stubbing out his roll-up and declaring there is further shopping to be done; he's hoping to track down "a pair of spaz-hot trainers" he spotted in a window yesterday.

And with that he's off, riding into the sunset. The last true movie star.

nowbiter must-haves

Quick on the draw: Chillum Holsters

Finally, a stylish way of carrying your chronic. With legalisation surely
just around the corner (we know you're reading, David Blunkett), the
designers at O-rangutan have come up with the very latest in skunk style,
with their range of Eighth-Wonder Chillum Holsters. Available in calf-skin and
panda fur, the pouches come adorned with an array of ironic prints, including
Bunny Wailer, a cancerous lung, and a rail crash. Currently only available in
London and Milan, these low-slung hipsters are bound to be a massive hit for tokers
who can handle a massive hit. Anyone for a big smoke in the big smoke?

Eighth-Wonder Chillum Holsters available at Kimono, retail £129.99

VITAL STATISTICS: Photo-ten-photo

Who? **Randall Jinx and Wuwu Poe**

Where? **Iceland**

What do Photo–ten–photo do? **Photo–ten–photo spit milk and blood over their unique range of hyper–erotic underwear.**

Why? **Because at £500 a vest and pant set, you expect something more for your money.**

Best Quote **Randall: 'My head is a great big karaoke machine.'**
Wuwu: 'I have never eaten a vegetable. I eat only meat and sawdust.'

Photo-ten-photo underwear is available from
Pylon Cripple, 99 Saturn Street, Reykjavik .

REBEL, YELL:

15 seconds with... Jason Thorkwell

27-year-old artist Jason Thorkwell is making a splash with his current
exhibition *Cum and Get It*. Visitors are provided with black
T-shirts, then asked to sit on a stool in front of a
small hatch, through which Thorkwell
masturbates, staining their chests with his
semen. Previously soiled shirts adorn the
walls of the exit corridor.
"Each one is unique; like a monochrome
Pollock rendered in glue," sniffs Thorkwell. We
asked him to fill out the nowbiter questionnaire.

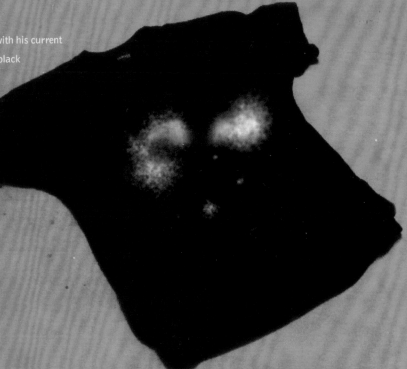

What are your influences? **Boris Pasternak. The stench of the Northern Line. Bowie. Microsoft. Lenny Henry. All artists. Fucking.**

What have you just been doing? **In all honesty? I've just been fucking.**

What are you going to do next? **Read Art Spiegelman's comic strip biography of Walpole.**

Where and when were you happiest? **Working on a building site in 1993.**

When did you last shed a tear? **1998, Modesto, CA: watching a Taco Bell sign fritz out at 3am.**

Describe your work in four words **Paradoxical. Straightforward. Black. White.**

What is over-rated? **So-called arts journalism.**

How would you like to die? **In a revolution.**

Really? **No.**

Cum and Get It is at the Nixon Gallery for the next three weeks. Admission costs £57.90 and does not include the cost of the T-shirt.

BOX KICKER

Sam Abbotson kicks a Tupperware box around. "Yesterday I kicked it down there," she says, indicating a grey stretch of pavement. "Tomorrow I might kick it past Dixon's."

Abbotson has been kicking boxes now for "six months, maybe more", and doesn't intend to stop any time soon. "I don't have anything else to do", she says, "and besides, it's fun."

Not everyone agrees. In May one old lady was so enraged  by Abbotson's box-kicking she muttered under her breath and scowled. Abbotson found the over-reaction baffling.

"Was she upset? I've no idea why."

Since then, acclaim for her work has poured in, but for the meantime at least, the 24-year-old is keeping

Mile High

Going "fluuuuurrrrrrrgggghhhh"
Still going "blaaaaaaagggghhh"? Pah.

K'zus
The 21st Century kazoo you attach to your hip via a keychain.

Playing the *Minder* theme on your K'zu
Altogether now: "Ah could be so goo fo yoo..." Priceless.

Glow-in-the-dark Japanese toothbrushes that make kissing sounds when you raise them to your lips
We bought ours on the internet two month ago.

Chaz Panther
Seen THAT video yet? We have, obviously. Ker-lassic.

Face Flags
They's a-gonna be HUGE, Massah Johnson

Ibsen 9Z-10

CLUB SILENCE

Club Silence is revolutionising our concept of a good night out. And it doesn't even exist. 'Everyone's a collectividual,' says its founder, Josh Thirteen.

You can't stand in the corner of Club Silence because it doesn't have one. You can't leave because there aren't any doors. You can't enter for precisely the same reason. Face it; you're already there. 'Since I can remember,' begins skater-turned-writer-turned-film-maker-turned-shop-assistant who used to polish glass shelves on which stood £500 fisherman's hats, Josh Thirteen, 'people have believed that going clubbing means going to a club. How wanked up is that? Club Silence is happening everywhere, every minute of the day, and it's as cool as fuck.'

At 23, Josh is no stranger to being in his early twenties, and it's this same awareness of the blindingly obvious that gives him the edge over his contemporary non-creators. 'People aren't slogans...' He takes another swig from a can of Top Deck, and then he's off again, thoughts racing faster than a coked jockey (and coked horse). 'I used to walk around with this factory special Manhattan Portage urban support system with "Attitude" blazed across it. It was totally empty, and when people looked inside they were like... fucked.'

Club Silence is the first space to totally engage with the concept of non-ness. No building, no music, no bar, and best of all, no closing time. 'We're all in this together,' spits Josh, 'individuals don't exist anymore, and neither do collectives. We're a singular mass of collectividuals and we embrace the robotic above the humanistic. Life has become a totality of mechanisation and by repeatedly offering nothing I'm giving none of us everything.' You sure fucking are Josh, and thank fucking fuck.

EXTINCTION SEX NOW

APE MUTINEERS POP THE ACTIVIST CHERRY

Photography: NATHAN BARLEY, Stylist: PHOENIX FOSSINGTON

Odin wears:
Top by Lamb Potato, £110
Belt by L.O.O.T.R, £80
Jeans by Nosing Up The Hairtrigger, £450
Trainers by Prof. Wallingford, £310

Dan wears:
Shirt by Sam Motorway, £65
Aberfan effect trousers by Stainpipe, £150
Anklet by Rollerball On DVD, £15

Stenton wears:
Nosebag by The Oklahoma Face Satchel Company, £45
Rim pelmet by Sagtwister, £45
Soluble footware by Fizzpubble Useless, £125
Tooth glove by Hole Corporation, £125

FRIDAY

TV Terrestrial

Our Father Who Art in Chegwin: this passes for the face of a deity in *Cheggers Plays God*

Worthy Gawps

Cheggers Plays God
8.00pm TVGH 1

It was 1980, and a wave of cultural experimentation was sweeping the globe. Thor Heyerdahl sailed the Pacific in the *Kon-Tiki*, Erno Rubik invented the Rubik's Snake, Malcolm McLaren danced the Double Dutch and television producer Ponceton McCockbox wasn't going to be left behind.

McCockbox's brainwave was to raise 12 children in the Brazilian rainforest to believe Keith Chegwin was a deity. 'I'd had the idea a few years before,' remembers McCockbox, glancing at the legs of a waitress and giving a dejected sigh. 'But I couldn't find the right person to play God. 'Kevin Keegan, Henry Cooper, John Selwyn-Gummer, I tried them all,' mutters McCockbox, knocking back a large G&T. 'But then I saw Keith on a Swaporama in Norfolk – King's Lynn I think it was –

and you could see all these young people staring up at him, offering him gifts of electronic racing games and spirograph, and as Darts kicked off 'Boys From New York City' I shouted to my ex-wife – 'That's him! That's my God!'

The experiment was overseen by a team of 40 from Bristol University's Anthropology Department and incorporated the input of more than 200 sociologists, psychologists and theologians worldwide. 'Of course,' slurs McCockbox, 'then it all turned to bloody shit: twenty years in the bloody jungle, twenty years surrounded by bloody babies and bloody Chegwin bloody giggling and doing that funny inhaling noise he makes all the bloody time and not so much as one bloody shag in twenty bloody years. Bloody hell, what a bloody waste of time. The whole bloody thing.'

Josh Victorian

Gross-Out Night
7.30pm TVGH 2

American teenagers: you either love them or hate them. And if you love them, you're wrong.

Tonight TVGH 2 panders to the needs of any homesick US teens currently on our shores with a night of shows designed to make them punch the air and call their television a 'dude'.

If you want to fit in, here's how to behave like an American teenager: spend fifteen years being raised in unbelievable luxury in the most affluent nation on Earth, then plop a baseball cap on your head, whine about your parents, poke a middle finger up at innocent bystanders, indulge in witless vandalism with your snot-nosed gurgling pals, then go home and jig around your absurdly large bedroom listening to over-produced nu-metal shit in which a billion-dollar rockstar covered in conformo-regulatory tattoos and piercings throws a petulant tantrum on your behalf. Pricks.

Hammond Organ

101 Amazing facts

78. In separate incidents in 1998, four teenagers set dogs on fire and hurled them from their bedroom windows, claiming that a newsreader had instructed them to do so during a sports' round-up. Having viewed the broadcast in question, Scotland Yard cleared the newsreader of any blame, stating, 'all this man did was read a couple of ice-hockey scores, and that's no reason to burn a hound.'

79. The most repeated programme on British TV is a 1973 episode of *Columbo* in which Leonard Nimoy did it.

80. Research has shown it is impossible to watch a television show on a bright summer's afternoon without becoming melancholic about your school days.

TV GH 1

9.30am Daily Mail Island
Another edition of the astounding social experiment in which volunteers are stranded on a remote island without access to any form of media other than the *Daily Mail*.
Week 22. Since arriving on the island, Roy has read nothing but the *Fred Bassett* comic strip, and has alienated the remaining islanders by perpetually standing on all fours in the corner of the communal living room silently interpreting mundane domestic events from the perspective of a whimsical cartoon hound stranded somewhere between 1958 and 1976.
Producer Dee Stopian *Subtitles.......888*

10.45 New Series
Look at the Tiger. Look at the Fucking Tiger. Stop Picking Your Nose and Look at the Fucking Tiger. It Took Us Ages to Film This, so the Least You Ungrateful Little Cuntsniffs Could Do is to Pay Some Fucking Attention for Once, Instead of Sitting There Slurping Your Fucking Sunny Delight and Fiddling With Your Shoelaces. Got That? Good: Now Stop Crying and Look at the Tiger, and You'd Better KEEP Fucking Looking at it or I'll Come Round and Belt-Whip You Into the Oblivion Ward of the Nearest Fucking Hospital, OKAY?
Explicitly confrontational version of *The Really Wild Show*.
Producer Lemonsip Toothpick *Subtitles...888*

TV GH 2

10.00am You Gay Fag
Real-life coming-out story of Simon Taylor, who lives in the small town of Ilkeston. This week Simon is made to say he likes hairy bums by the school bully, who then breaks his nose for liking hairy bums.
Producer Mikki Lowdown *Subtitles...888*

11.30 Tekken
Soap opera. Having seen off Yoshimitsu, Kazuya must confront Armor King. Paul and Roger decide to settle their differences atop a Hong Kong skyscraper.
Producer John Heck *Subtitles...888*

12.30pm Don't Repeat the Past Participle!
Smug parlour game with a vague right-wing hue hosted by Alan Coren, in which self-satisfied micro celebrities demonstrate correct grammar for points. Today's team captains are Tony Slattery and Jean Boht.
Producer Marge Pott *Subtitles...888*

2.45 S Club 7's Self-Assembly Hospital Furniture Blockjam
The feisty teenage pop group hold a street party to perform some of their favourite songs while assembling a variety of flat-pack MDF shelving units for use in a nearby children's hospital.
Producer Kate Outtahere *Poptitles...888*

3.20 New Series
Barbara Ellen Solves Mankind
New series in which axe-grinding *Observer* columnist Barbara Ellen orbits the planet perched atop an immense jet-propelled throne, using her devastating insight and coruscating wit to shatter all existing male preconceptions, thereby forcing every single man alive to finally recognise and confront his own fathomless chauvinism and subconscious misogyny.
Producer Giant Tits *Subtitles...888*

TV GH 3

9.25am Jakki Shelf
'Is that a Ladbrokes? It looks like a Ladbrokes But I Can't Tell From Here. All These Betting Shops Are So Similar Aren't They? Is it a Ladbrokes? It's a William Hill You Say? Oh. Well It Looked Like a Ladbrokes'.
Producer Alan Punk *Subtitles...888*

10.00 Chatroom
Soap opera. Jake16 enters, says hi folks :) wassup? Mizz T sends big kissys xxxxx hiya jakester hows trix!? Thomas has left the chatroom.
Producer BB Tymewaste *Subtitles...888*

11.30 Omni Logo News
Nike Swoosh and the Starbucks Mermaid usher in VT reports jam-packed with gunfire and bloodshed.
Producer Alma Geddon *Subtitles...888*

12.30pm Condorman Fucks Up
Piloting a 737 high above New York on Christmas Eve, Condorman disengages the autopilot and attempts to fly beneath the Brooklyn Bridge in order to impress a stewardess.
Producer Jinks Casey *Subtitles...888*

2.00 Indiana Jones and the Doomed Office Romance
5. Dr Jones strikes up an ostensibly jokey correspondence with Karen using the company's internal email system, but their exchange ends abruptly when she fails to respond to an overtly flirtatious message sent in a flurry of misguided excitement, leaving the erstwhile explorer crushed and despairing.
Producer K.Y. Silly *Subtitles....888*

3.25 Film Premiere
Saving Primate Ryan
Acclaimed Spielberg war epic re-enacted by the chimpanzees from the popular series of PG Tips television commercials.
Director Steven Spielberk *Subtitles...888*

TV GH 4

9.30am Puppet Funerals
Obsolete TV puppets laid to rest in a series of moving ceremonies. This week: 'Mooncat' from erstwhile children's show *Get Up and Go* makes his final television appearance.
Producer Jenny Tesco *Subtitles...888*

12.30pm Cranial Intrusion Afternoon
Gorden Kaye introduces a smattering of programmes revolving around the violation of the human skull.

12.45 Trepanny Peck
Andre Agassi stars as the hard-bitten New York detective whose attempts at crime-solving are perpetually hindered by a woodpecker nipping at his brain through a gaping hole in his forehead. *The Killer Wore Fish Canoes*. On the trail of a professional hitman, Peck finds himself struggling to make sense of the most basic clues as the woodpecker drills through his memory banks and powers of reason.
Producer Shakatak Jones *Subtitles...888*

1.40 Headbake Castle
Jenny Powell introduces the ground-breaking quiz show in which contestants don a microwave helmet that slowly cooks their brains while they answer quickfire general knowledge questions until the power of speech deserts them and an overweight man dressed as a cartoon bear cajoles them into running across a plank carrying a bucket of water.
Producer Dan Frank *Subtitles...888*

2.10 Forehead Darts
Incredibly dangerous version of the popular pub game.
Producer Sid Parrott *Subtitles...888*

2.50 Allez Pour Le Cerveau
Off-beat French series in which schoolchildren jab wooden skewers into the tearducts of convicted murderers in a bid to pierce the brain and induce involuntary muscle spasms in time to whirling accordion music for comic effect.
Producer Serge Versailles *Soobteetles...888*

REGIONAL VARIATIONS

PRISON

6.00pm Scenes From Out There

6.25 Uninterrupted Snooker from 1979

9.00 Lights Out

CRASHING PLANE

6.25pm Turbulence

6.30 Sinister Bang

6.32 Plummet

6.33 Brace Brace Screaming

6.34 Closedown

2.00am Black Box Recovery

8.00pm In Keith we trust: the children raised to worship Chegwin

6.00pm Post-Coital News
Up-to-the-minute current affairs read by a thoroughly satiated couple sporting damp matted hair and sticky chins and chests.
Producer Alma Geddon   *Subtitles...888*

7.30 Don't Look
Horror. People being interviewed for current affairs and arts programmes steal unnerving sideways glances at the camera, as though they've suddenly spotted you watching them.
Producer Damon Green   *Subtitles...888*

8.00 New Series
Cheggers Plays God
Fascinating sociological experiment for the television age. In 1982 twelve abandoned babies were flown to a specially-constructed village in the thick of the Amazonian rainforest. Totally isolated from the rest of the world, they have been raised to accept Keith Chegwin as their God. From his gold-plated observation tower in the centre of the village, the pudgy-faced manchild uses a combination of hidden cameras and state-of-the-art technology to control the hearts and minds of his people as they begin to give birth to a second generation of 'Chegwinites'.
Producer Ponceton McCockbox   *Subtitles...888*

11.30 We Done Had a Row
Live call-in show in which Anne Robinson fields inarticulate mobile phone calls from drunken proletarian males who've just held bitter post-pub arguments with their girlfriends.
Attention all proles: have you just stood in the street having a loud pointless disagreement with your girlfriend, accusing her of fancying someone else while she repeatedly shrieked her ignorance? Will it all be forgotten by this time tomorrow, when you lazily squirt two bollockfuls of lukewarm plebspunk up her slack crimson flue, so that nine months later she can contribute to Britain's ever-rising Scum Mountain by firing an entirely unnecessary rat-eyed infant out of her cunt – a hot-faced mewling little monster the pair of you can bicker and moan about for years to come, until it eventually develops into a spiteful teenage dogboy who spends every Friday night roaming the streets of an ugly market town searching for things to break or fight or fuck in a reckless bid to purge itself of just one percent of the shit and bile and stagnant fury you've been filling it with since the day it was born? The We Done Had a Row team are waiting for your call: dial 0207 946 0005 now.
Producer Damien Thorn   *Subtitles...888*

12.30am Mick Hucknall's Pink Pancakes
Mick strolls the length of Blackpool's 'Golden Mile' clad only in a tight transparent macintosh.
Producer Minnie Stootighttomention   *Subtitled...888*

7.30pm The US of Asshole: hateful American teens get a night of their own

7.00pm Gandalf in Calais
Having defeated the dark power of Sauron, Gandalf Greyhame decides to take advantage of a cheap ferry offer in the *Daily Mail*. But he little suspects a wrong turn on the autoroute will leave him driving round and round the Calais one-way system at 2am in a car full of clanking bottles...
Producer Damon Green   *Subtitles...888*

7.30 Gross-Out Night
An evening of tiresome shit designed to amuse snotty US male teenagers.

7.35 Like, Duhhh
Outrageous stunt show in which sniggering frat boys torment genuinely retarded people by running up behind them, tapping them on one shoulder, then darting to the other side as they turn around. Music by Limp Bizkit.
Producer Alvin Krack   *Subtitles...888*

8.50 Yo, Why Should I Give a Fuck About Anything?
Home-video footage of spoilt US teens hurling bags of shit through the windows of passing cars. Music by Limp Bizkit.
Producer Jack Shitt   *Subtitles...888*

9.20 Best of Spring Break Whooping
A full uninterrupted hour of obnoxious American cunts rolling their fists in the air, hooting and bellowing while dim cheerleaders pop their tops. Music by Limp Bizkit.
Producer Bud Titties   *Subtitles...888*

10.10 Dude, I Barfed Up Your Ass
'Gross-out' comedy starring Fred Durst as Dick Sakk, a college drop-out who accidentally swallows his mother's wedding ring, then vomits it up a friend's anus as part of a drunken bet. With his parents' anniversary looming, Dick must follow his friend around, carefully examining everything that emerges from his backside for an entire month...
Dick Sakk...FRED DURST
Pussy Popper.................................CARMEN ELECTRA
Dweezil Asswipe............................JOHNNY KNOXVILLE
Director Mack Baddy (1999, 15)   *Subtitles...888*

12.30am Cunt
Nathan Barley stands in the queue of a Clerkenwell soup bar waiting to pay £4.95 for a cardboard cupful of coconut frankfurter chowder while loudly discussing *The Sopranos* with a skeletal girl in a patterned sarong and a pastel blue t-shirt with the words 'Dicktoy Slut' emblazoned ironically across her chest in the style of the Cadbury's Dairy Milk logo.
Producer Lo-Slung Denim   *Subtitles...888*

TV GH 3

10.00pm Doodle or die: only the funniest goose sketcher will survive

7.30pm New Series
Vague Recollection Moviehouse
Big-budget series in which well-known movies are remade according to scripts written by members of the public attempting to recollect the story and dialogue as accurately as possible despite only having seen the original version once, several years previously.
1. Cliffhanger. Sylvester Stallone stars as a mountain climber who accidentally drops a woman down a canyon and gets chased around in the snow by a bunch of terrorists led by the round-faced man from *Third Rock From The Sun.*
Gabe Something...SYLVESTER STALLONE
Canyon Drop Woman...................................SANDRA BULLOCK
Old Man...THINGY WALTON
Main Terrorist...............................THIRD ROCK FROM THE SUN MAN
Another Terrorist...........................DAN FROM EASTENDERS
Producer Jinks Casey   *Subtitles...888*

9.30 Police! Press Conference! Breakdown!
Fascinating sobbing-relative action is the order of the day as Steve Penk introduces a selection of the most compellingly tragic moments ever captured by the unflinching gaze of the modern news media.
Do you think grieving relatives look funny? Would you like to see them flogged in public? Are you prepared to air ludicrously unpopular views like this on national television? The Kilroy team would like to speak to you. Call now on 020 7946 0002.
Producer David Shark   *Subtitles...888*

10.00 Fun Goose or War
Edge-of-the-seat gameshow in which two ageing bachelors are flown over an African warzone and commanded to draw a cartoon goose on the back of a shovel with a lump of coal. The creator of the most amusing sketch is slowly fellated by a prostitute with a mouthful of honey, while the loser parachutes into the middle of the raging battle below, armed only with a dustbin lid, a clockwork pistol and a webcam glued to his forehead.
Producer Janice Biscuits   *Subtitles...888*

10.45 Wife in the Next Room
Reasoning that his wife must come out at night to go to the toilet, Darren sets up a deckchair in the hallway, and waits for her to emerge – to be woken at 4am by a bleeping robot carrying a bucket of urine, and watching, slack-jawed, as it tips it over his head and returns to the rapidly-locked kitchen.
Producer Log Nonymous   *Subtitles...888*

TV GH 4

2.00am Wahey! Boring drug-addled fucks jigging around with their eyes bulging out

7.30pm TuneyWatch 2000
Elongated scattercast of music-scented programmes whispered into position by Jo Whiley and Axl Rose.

7.35 Goat's Throat Bandstand
Continuing the unconventional music series in which popular bands attempt to play their greatest hits using rudimentary kazoo-style instruments constructed from a goat's larynx stuck on the end of a drinking straw.
4. The Manic Street Preachers visit the Castleton leisure centre in Edinburgh to perform songs including *A Design for Life, Everything Must Go, Australia,* and *If You Tolerate This Your Children Will Be Next.*
Producer Leonard Tripwire   *Subtitles...888*

9.05 Skunk Plugger
Fly-on-the-wall documentary following the life of Mike Yacht, a weasel-eyed music industry plugger whose main duties include manhandling female teen-pop acts, supplying cocaine to influential radio DJs, and scampering through nightclubs, recording studios, brothels and restaurants like a hideous scrawny axe-faced rat.
1. Yacht takes an illicit digital photo of a 19-year-old chart singer's arsecrack as she lies unconscious on a hotel bed caked in piss, puke, spittle and coke, before sitting on the floor for a chemically-enhanced stoneface wank to the in-house soft porn channel.
Producer Harold Barley   *Subtitles...888*

11.15 Deathbed LullaByeBye Karaoke Chorus
Moving experimental show in which members of the viewing public sing onscreen lyrics into their telephones and have their voices collated into a single haunting nationwide choir, performing tender lullabies to terminal patients whose dying moments are relayed live on air.
Producer Peter Out   *Subtitles...888*

2.00am New Series
Latenite ClubbaMental
Magazine programme looking at the world of music written for people on drugs by composers on drugs, consisting of interviews with DJs on drugs conducted by a female presenter on drugs and punctuated by footage of bug-eyed dancers on drugs shot by a flailing cameraman on drugs and later edited in time with the music by an editor on drugs acting on the orders of an overweight and confused producer on drugs, whose show (the proceeds from which are spent immediately on drugs) is broadcast in the dead of night where it goes unnoticed by everyone except viewers on drugs. *Caution: watching this programme makes you a cunt.*
Producer Brian Nostrils   *Gurning subtitles...888*

DIGITAL, SATELLITE AND CABLE

KEY CUTTER MAX

9.00am Non-Stop Yale Buffing Party

12.00pm Key Fobs Of The Stars

1.00 Re-Heeled But Never Collected Anecdotes

2.00 The Inspector Chubb Mysteries

4.00 Deadlock P.I.

5.00 Padlock of the Yard

6.00 Rubber Heels

7.00 Dog Tag MD

8.00 Bolt From The Blue

9.00 Keyring Investigates

10.00 The Police Constable Keycutter Casebook

12–4am Keycutter Academy
How to cut keys, re-heel shoes, engrave dog collars, and flirt with young women whilst wearing a dirty old apron and fiddling with greasy machinery.

INFIDELITY GOLD

The channel for those who suspect their partner is having an affair.

9.00am Open Forum
Is she wearing perfume to work?

10.00 Wedding Vows
Thou shall not commit adultery

11.00 Rod, Jane And Freddy

12.00pm The Things Kids Say!
Why Does Daddy Always Work Late?

2.00 Games For Two
Swapping mobile phone bills and guessing who the unfamiliar numbers belong to.

3.00 Dustin Hoffman Double Bill
Introduced by Mick Jagger and Jerry Hall.

3.05 The Graduate

4.45 Kramer Versus Kramer

7.00 Britain's Biggest Cuckolds

8.00 Butterflies

8.30 Duty Free

11.00 Where the Fuck Is She?

12–3am Row Zone Pop
More great songs to drown out the sounds of shouting and tears. Includes Gladys Knight and the Tindersticks.

CRAYON MAGNATE EXTREME

The only satellite channel that caters for those who like to pretend they're heir to a coloured crayon empire

7.00am Business Breakfast
Updates on crayon market share and sales projections.

9.00 Point Of View Golf
A round with the son of a toilet tissue magnate.

11.00 Window Shopper
Sloane Street.

12.00pm Gawping At Workers

1.00 Paternal Reprimand
3. It's time you bucked your ideas up and focused more on the crayon business.

2.00 Let's Confess!
5. I can get any girl I want to tongue the end of my lazy prick just by mentioning my position within a coloured crayon empire and it's starting to get really boring.

3.00 Closedown Siesta

9.00 Jerk Off To This
A maid sorts through a holdall of your dirty sportsgear.

10.00 Crayons Today

12–7am Sweet Slumber
Coloured crayons swirl around the screen to the sound of chinging cash registers

LOWBROW ARTHOUSE MOVIEPIPE

The cinema channel that simultaneously insults your intelligence and goes clean over your head.

3.20pm Indiana Jones and the Portuguese Widow

5.45 Look Who's Quoting Rousseau

7.30 Honey, I Recontextualised the Kids

9.10 Police Academy XI: Power Without Responsibility?

10.55 The Unbearable Muppetness of Being

12.10am Dude, What's the Point?

CLASSIC INTERROGATION ONE

For those who crave the thrill and desperation of a high pressure police interrogation.

6.00am Oi Wake the Fuck Up

6.05 Now Drink This

6.10 Jesus, He's Shit All Down His Strides

6.20 Not So Hard Now Are We?

6.30 Staring at Clouds Behind Bars

6.45 Meet the Scotsman

7.00 Flashback
Running through the garden as a child, clutching a toy car, gurgling for joy.

7.10 Start the Tape

7.20 Say Nothing

7.30 Stop the Tape

7.40 Blackeyes

8.40 Start the Tape II

9.00 Memory Loss

10.00 Phone a Friend

11.00 Make It Easy On Yourself

12.00pm Did You See Mark In The Car Park?

1.00 Flashback
Walking home from school with a girl with the most beautiful smile in the world.

1.05 What Was the Question?

1.10 Did You See Mark in the Car Park?

1.20 Stare at Your Fingers

1.25 Did You See Mark in the Car Park?

1.30 Deep Sigh

1.35 Did You See Mark in the Car Park?

1.40 Regret

1.45 Did You See Mark in the Car Park?

1.50 Gaze at the Wall

1.55 Did You See Mark in the Car Park?

2.00 Did You See Mark in the Car Park?

2.10 Did You See Mark in the Car Park?

2.15 We've Got All Day – Now Did You or Did You Not See Mark in the Car Park?

2.20 Ouch!

2.25 Did You See Mark in the Car Park?

2.30 Arrggghh!

2.35 Did You See Mark in the Car Park?

2.40 Did You See Mark in the Car Park?

2.43 DID YOU SEE MARK IN THE CAR PARK?

2.44 Leave Me Alone

2.45 Well Did You? Did You See Him? Don't Fuck us About

2.46 Did You See Mark in the Car Park?

2.47 Please God

2.48 Did You See Mark in the Fucking Car Park?

2.55 Please God Make it Stop

2.56 DID YOU SEE MARK IN THE CAR PARK?

2.57 Can't Open Mouth Can't Open It Don't Say Don't Say Can't Open Mouth Can't

2.59 DID YOU SEE MARK IN THE CAR PARK?

3.00 Now I Remember

4.00 Sign Here

4.10 Flashback
Dancing on your father's knee, as an uncle with fingers that smell of fag smoke ruffles your hair and says 'He'll be the brains of this family'.

4.15 Just Sign

4.20 Flashback
A January morning, walking in the snow.

4.30 Sign Your Name

4.40 Flashback
Drawing spiders on your plimsolls in biro.

5.00 Put Pen To Paper

5.30 Within These Walls

6.00 Through The Peep Hole

7.00 Darkness

8.00 Distant Sound Of Traffic

9.00 Tearing Sheets

10.00 Stool Challenge

11.00 Flashback
Chasing flies through shafts of light in the summer time.

12.00am Kick

12.05 Swing

12.10 Eternal Closedown

Flushed in space: zero gravity trouble for Ralph Fiennes in *Widdleplop III: Destination Mars*

MOVIE CHOICE

7.20pm Every (Every Single Day, Every Single Day, Every Single) Day That I'm Without You (Hurts a Little Bit) Hurts (a Little Bit) Just a Little Bit More (Just a Little More) Than (Just a Little More) I've Ever Been Hurt Before

Romantic drama based on the Sad Café song 'Everyday Hurts', starring Steve Guttenberg as a man who, having seen the lamp light from her window, asks his former lover why she'd had to hurt him so – and why it was she

Had to go.

Away.

Hurt Guy..................STEVE GUTTENBERG
Lamplight Window Girl..DARYL HANNAH
Young Man Across the Street, He Looks Something Like Me, And He's Walking With His Head Down To The Ground........................GRIFFIN DUNNE
Director Melody Nelson (1983, PG)
Subtitles...888

8.50 Premiere
Honey, I Browndicked an Acrobat

Shocking and bizarre comedy starring **Rick Moranis** as an eccentric suburban inventor who, having plugged his brain into a 'mind magnifier' of his own creation, wakes to find himself inexplicably sodomising a circus performer in an antique bath.

Wayne Szalinski..................RICK MORANIS
Mitch the Incredible.............RICK WITTER
Director Harold Yamgut (1985, 15)
Subtitles...888

11.30 Last Play
Yo! Diary of Anne Frank

Energetic musical based on the moving diaries, composed by and starring European pop supergroup **Aqua**. Includes the songs *Warehouse Warehouse Hideaway* and *Badtime Fascist Christmas*.

Anne Frank................................LENE
Bouncy Guy.............................RENE
Snooping Neighbour.......................CLAUS
Whistleblower.........................SOREN
Director Tor Nosebleed (1998, PG)
Subtitles...888

1.30am Premiere
Widdleplop III: Destination Mars

Wilfully sickening sci-fi starring Ralph Fiennes. Wearying of his continual ordure-oriented misfortune on Earth, cattle farmer Harold Walsh constructs a rocket ship, fills it with livestock and blasts off into space in a bid to establish a new farm on Mars. But disaster strikes when an accidental meteor collision ruptures the valves of the craft's sanitation system, sending raw effluence pumping into the capsule – in turn triggering an outbreak of violent bovine stomach disorders, leaving his herd vomiting, urinating and spraying hot diarrhoea in zero gravity. With Walsh trapped helplessly within, the spacecraft, by now completely filled to the brim with fetid waste, is doomed to orbit Mars for an eternity, like a big white bottle of shit bobbing around in a surreal black ocean. *Contains explicit close-ups of cows' red raw ringpieces, burning like a hot coin, belching clouds of shit into the uncomprehending emptiness of space.*
Harold Walsh.....................RALPH FIENNES
Director Peter Jackson (2001, 15)

81. In France, there is just one police uniform available for hire by TV production companies. As a result, most of the buttons are hanging off the shirt and the trousers are thin at the knees.

82. Cultural analysts believe that if Hitler had been born in 1976, he might now be president of the *Only Fools and Horses* fan club and drive around in a yellow Robin Reliant in homage to the show.

83. A woman died while being gunged on the Spanish gameshow *Hot Uniform!* As her husband ran from the crowd to cradle his wife's custard-soaked body, the director sent on a troop of dancing midgets to present him with a digital alarm clock featuring the show's logo.

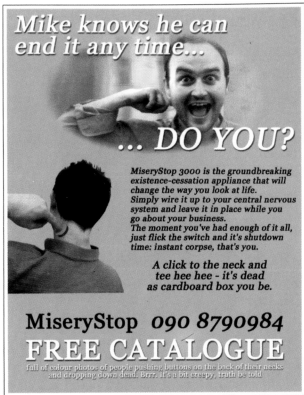

The TV of
Tomorrow

The shows we watch on it may remain the same, but the television itself is perpetually evolving. First there was the innovation of full colour broadcasts. Then came portable TV, closely followed by the remote control. More recently, sleek, wide plasma-screen sets have become an everyday sight, provided you're obscenely rich.

So what does the TV of tomorrow have to offer? Find out now as we stare inquisitively into the crystal ball of the future…

① Holographic head
This helpful virtual assistant is on hand to slowly rotate in the centre of the living room, reminding the occupants they are living in the future.

② Scrolling news ticker
Provides continuous updates from the world of current affairs. In event of impending nuclear war, ticker displays light-hearted philosophical quotations designed to make inhabitants view their forthcoming extinction in a humorous context.

③ Nacho cannon
Fires nacho chips directly into viewer's face during broadcasts. Firing rate increases during tense or arousing scenes. Optional ceiling outlet can be programmed to drip three different brands of salsa onto chip as it sails in mid-air.

④ Family member cam
Causes family members to appear on screen, digitally inserted as background extras, thereby negating viewer's occasional desire to turn head and see them for real in order to remember what they look like.

⑤ Lightgun
Enables viewer to blast at crudely demonised hate figures during news broadcasts.

⑥ Trough
Collects inevitable tears of self-loathing.

Once full, trough may be drained and tears used to form base of cooking sauces.

⑦ Cynical sofa-bound sidekick automaton
Supplies side-splitting and subversive one-liners effectively mocking everything on screen until viewer laughs themselves unconscious, at which point it gently whispers advertising slogans into their ear.

⑧ Domestic blimp
Slowly circumnavigates room, displaying official Government orders.

⑨ Leg clamp
Prevents viewer from missing favourite shows by getting up and leaving. Size adjustable to suit all age groups.

⑩ Lying window
Technologically-advanced exterior landscape interface designed to make outdoor world appear threatening and unfair, thereby rendering indoor hovel instantly cosy by way of comparison. Digital imaging technology simulates inclement weather, blade-wielding miscreants, rampaging monsters and sinister floating bacterial spores on the fly.

⑪ High definition display screen
Delivers images twice as sharp as real-life counterparts. Built-in picture enhancement system automatically airbrushes blemishes from faces of celebrities while simultaneously converting all varieties of skin tone to universal Caucasian hue.

⑫ Thought hoover
Retrieves semi-conscious thoughts on possible means of improving current broadcast directly from viewer's mind and carries them to in-box of junior marketing research trainee based in sinister Hounslow megaplex shaped like five-pointed star.

⑬ CCTV goldfish
Sophisticated spy-cam disguised as live goldfish peers relentlessly at occupants of living room for no particular reason besides routine invasion of privacy.

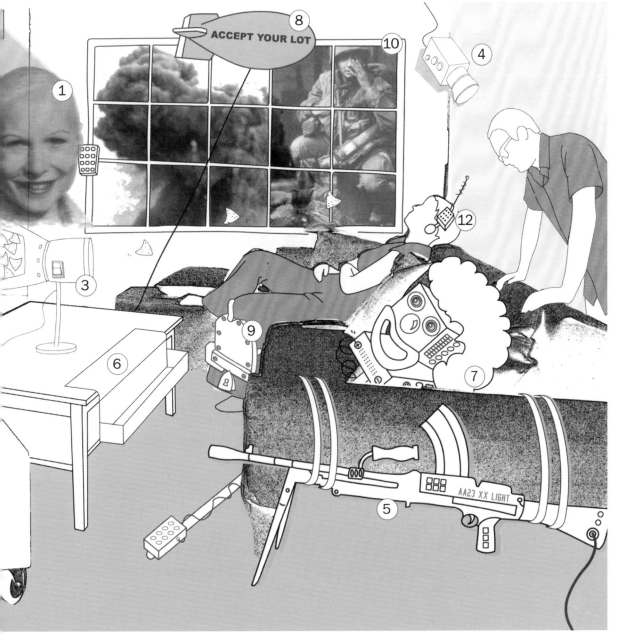

The Ins and Outs of
Shittiquette
A guide to crapping away from home

When Michael Stipe sang 'Everybody Hurts' he may as well have been singing 'Everybody Shits' instead. Because everybody – everybody – has to go to the lavatory now and again. From the lowliest tramp to the starriest princess – all have to strain their bowels before sundown. Defecation may be a perfectly natural bodily function, but that doesn't mean you want to draw attention to it. Crapping is an intensely private pastime, and consequently few things are as nerve-wracking as having to 'go' away from home. Whether it be in a workplace washroom, or at your partner's parents' house, a stranger's lavatory is rarely inviting. Now, as TVGH1 celebrates the world of bum eggs with *Bank Holiday Panblockers* (MONDAY, TVGH1), we've invited covert plop authority Steve Fence – author of *Going Undercover: The Art of Covert Shitting* – to bring you an expert guide to vacating your bowels in unfamiliar surroundings.

STEP ONE: Preparation

If you're determined to achieve undetected defecation, you can't just leap in and start blindly crapping away. First, you've got to tackle the groundwork. Before undertaking any kind of plopdown manoeuvre, the two most important issues to resolve

are when to go and where to do it. Obviously, you have no control over timing or location when trying to crap on a train or aircraft. If this is the case, the best you can do is achieve damage limitation by skipping step one completely and heading straight for step two.

The rest of you, follow me:

When to go

Timing is essential. It's no good ambling off to the lavatory whenever you feel like it. It's not your house, remember? You must choose your moment with the precision of a stealth assassin.

A key question to

ask is 'has anyone else used the toilet recently?' If the answer is YES, it's best to wait a few minutes for the sake of your own comfort.

If the answer is NO, attempt to ascertain the likelihood of

someone else wanting to use it in the immediate future – i.e. straight after you, when it's likely to smell. Look around you. Has anyone eaten recently? If you're in someone's home, are they settling down to watch a film? If you're at work, are they about to hold a meeting? Does anyone, even vaguely, look as though they might need a shit?

If you can't answer these questions to a satisfactory degree of accuracy, then you MUST bide your time. If at all possible, hold it in until you're back at home. If you're staying over at someone's house, wait until everyone else goes to bed – ideally they will have been tucked up for an hour or more by the time your cheeks hit the seat.

Where to go

Upon arrival, it is essential to familiarise yourself with the layout of the building. You should note how many toilets are available and where they are located. Also note which, if any, are situated within a full-blown bathroom and which are stand-alone units. If staying at someone else's house, do not pick a toilet on a busy thoroughfare. Nothing is worse than walking out of the toilet and bumping straight into someone's mother as a cloud of offensive shitfunk billows from the room behind you. The ideal location is as far away as possible rom everyone else in the building; or instance, if working in an office within a large building, try to use a oilet on a quiet, unfamiliar floor if at all possible.

f the only option open to you is a communal workplace toilet, pick a cubicle far away from the door. Always choose an end cubicle: NEVER enter a cubicle sandwiched between two others.

f you're staying with a family gathered in the living room watching television, seek out the uppermost toilet in the house – they may not even be aware of any flushing sounds, leaving your crap completely undetected. f you can locate a toilet in the same room as a bath or shower, then congratulations: you've hit the jackpot. Simply ask if it's okay if you have a bath, lock yourself in, run the taps, and lay cable to your heart's content. The bathtime dump is truly a dream come true: the noise of rushing water masks any noise you may be emitting (see Step Two for more on noise

elimination), and by the time you've finished pooing and had a soak in the tub, all stench will have dissipated (see Step Three for further information).

STEP TWO:
The Act Itself

Once ensconced on the throne your primary concern is noise. If you've picked your moment and location carefully (see Preparation) then toilet noise may not be an issue. In an ideal situation, you will be free to make as much racket as you like without fear of being overheard. Sometimes, however, circumstances dictate this is not the case. Small houses with a single bowl, workplace lavatories, and

shared guest house bathrooms are all potential danger spots – but with care, you can pass undetected. Toilet noise falls into one of two main categories: anal trumpeting and faecal splash. The good news is that these two sonic fields tend to be mutually exclusive: a stool turgid and weighty enough to produce a flamboyant sploshing sound is likely to have been expelled in relative silence, whilst the triumphant rasp of diarrhoea generally accompanies droplets of brown matter which gently spatter the sides of the bowl instead of plunging noisily into the seas below.

Whatever the sound you're making, keeping the decibel level to an absolute minimum should be your goal. Here are a few suggestions.

Reducing 'plungedown'

Place toilet paper in the bowl before evacuating your bowels. A small furl of two to three loosely-spooled sheets is ideal – this acts as a kind of 'sonic safety net', gently catching the plummeting stool and eliminating embarrassing splash sounds.

NB: DO NOT use an excess of paper to create your furl. You may block the pan altogether, causing overspill. If that happens for God's sake just hang yourself with your belt. It'll be easier for all concerned.

Masking anal rasping

A spluttering sphincter reverberating around a cavernous toilet bowl is one of the most humiliating sounds you can make with your body – and unfortunately it's often unavoidable, particularly if you've been holding in gas for some time in a bid to avoid passing wind in front of your hosts.

Your best course of action is to mask the din. Coughing in time to each eruption is effective, but something of a giveaway. Whistling or humming to yourself is inadvisable – it only draws unwelcome attention and makes you sound nervous.

If you have taken a newspaper into the toilet with you, rustle and turn the pages as demonstratively as you can. If there is a sink within arm's reach, run the tap. Don't set it to full blast – that's another giveaway; a gentle trickle should be sufficient to camouflage most quiet noises. Hot taps are most effective, as they often have the bonus side-effect of summoning up an obfuscating hubbub from the boiler and pipes. In extreme cases, where the anal noise is excessive and you're certain of being overheard unless urgent action is taken, it is acceptable to muffle the sound by clamping a piece of toilet paper against the mouth of your anus as wind is expelled. *Bear in mind this may leave you with shit on your hands.*

SHITTER'S TIP

Another way to reduce noise is to aim your exithole slightly to one side, so the falling stool lands against the wall of the bowl before sliding down to nestle softly in the base of the pan. Only use this method when there is a toilet brush to hand as it WILL cause streaking.

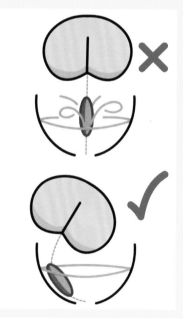

STEP THREE: Aftermath

You've chosen a good moment in a prime location, and no-one's heard a thing. Good work. But you're not out of the woods yet.

Now there's a new enemy to contend with: smell.

Smell is an inevitable by-product of defecation, and varies in tenor from 'light brown musk' to 'violent affront to human dignity'. The two main areas of concern here are minimising the smell at source, and then preventing others from encountering it. Let's take a look.

Minimising smell

The first rule of stench reduction is to act quickly – particularly in a situation where someone else is likely to be waiting to use the toilet. Do not dawdle once the waste has been expelled – flush the toilet immediately, prior to wiping. This may seem extreme, but it is an extremely effective means of minimising odour. Remember – better for someone outside to hear you flush twice (or even three times) than for them to walk in and catch a noseful of absolutely eye-watering bumsteam.

In situations where time is less of an issue, your options are varied. Family bathrooms often have a small window, which whenever possible should be opened to encourage the circulation of fresh air.

Striking a match to 'burn away' the smell can be helpful, but often leaves behind a tell-tale odour of its own. Many hosts thoughtfully place a canister of air-freshener in the bathroom. This should be approached with caution – the sound of the spray will immediately inform anyone within earshot that you're anxiously trying to conceal the reek from a massive log, and besides, the perfume itself is rarely sufficient to eradicate the smell. Indeed, if used carelessly, air-freshener can actually exacerbate your predicament by creating a heady cocktail of undesirable odours: the scent of synthetic lavender, in particular, can be spectacularly unpleasant when combined with the lingering remnants of a hot and pungent shit.

Preventing others from entering

With the arena of smell being so fraught with danger, by far the most effective way of avoiding embarrassment is to ensure nobody else will use the toilet for some time. In some circles it is socially acceptable to warn others you have left an odour behind immediately upon exit. Whilst this may be tolerable amongst a group of relative strangers of the same sex, it should only be used as a last resort – and should never be employed by anyone vacating a toilet on a bus, train, or aircraft. In situations where your absence may go unnoticed for up to twenty minutes, you may want to consider simply remaining inside the cubicle until the stench has dissipated. Be sure to take a book or magazine to read in with you beforehand. By far the most effective method of making the toilet a no-go area until the offending smell has receded is the bath poo method (see Preparation). That's truly a shit from heaven.

SHITTER'S TIP

Be sure to check the bowl for marks before leaving. No-one wants to walk into a lavatory after you, spot a tell-tale streak, and think 'ergh, that came from their arse'. Not even for a second.

Steve Fence's *Going Undercover: The Art of Covert Shitting* is available to buy from a wheel in the sky.

ZAPPING Incorporating Braying Wanker

MOBILE PRICK

I'M ON A BUS
Start stating the obvious today

DUM DEE DUM DEE DEE DUM
101 phone tunes only a sociopath would choose

BLAH BLAH BLAH
How to go on and on and on and on and on and on and on about your pointless fucking life

FREE KAZOO!
Annoy all within earshot without using your phone

January 2004
£3.95

Not for sale to anyone who isn't a grating piece of loudmouthed shit

---

SWANS ARE SHIT + + + SWANS ARE SHIT + + + SWANS ARE SHIT + + + SWANS ARE SHIT + + + SWANS ARE SHIT

SwanHater
The journal of cygnus detestation

Vol.1 No.6
Mar 2002

Watery SCUM
Tell those lakebound motherfuckers where to get off

SIGNET KICKING   EGG THEFT   POISONED LAKES   THOSE NECKS. WHY?

---

issue 43 Nov 2001 £2.99

ANICKING MURDERER
or crime-of-passion killers in a hur

BURIAL BUDDIES
Latest shovels reviewed and rated

IS THIS YOUR TIE, SIR?
Common cover-up errors you must avoid

WHAT HAVE I DONE?
Your 10-point guide to the immediate aftermath

FREE "EASY WAY OUT" CYANIDE PILL!
NOT AVAILABLE IN IRELAND. IS YOUR DEATH PILL MISSING? ASK YOUR NEWSAGENT!

---

practical soapeater

issue thirty-six
june 2004 £4.99

the six tastiest shampoos

delia's imperial leather recipes

britain's top soap cafes

mmm!
newest bars tasted and rated

foaming throat syndrome: the truth

pubes: the soap eater's wiry croutons

FREE FORK

101
Amazing television facts

84. If you place your head directly in front of a satellite dish you can feel QVC pass directly through your mind.

85. Moroccan trains have televisions in place of windows. To further disorientate passengers, the screens display images of landscape passing in the opposite direction.

86. Televisions come in two formats: economy and first class. First class TVs come complete with a stewardess who slings croissants into your lap during commercial breaks.

87. Old broadcasts drift out into space and get snagged on bits of interstellar debris. During a 1997 Space Shuttle mission, an astronaut glanced at a passing meteorite and was astonished to find an episode of *Scarecrow and Mrs King* snagged on its side.

88. Television can be slowed to half its normal speed by dipping the aerial in honey. This has another surprising side effect – it turns everyone on-screen bright orange.

89. The catchiest TV theme tune of all time accompanied a Canadian sitcom called *Ralph's In Trouble*. All who heard it were instantly rendered immobile for the rest of their lives as they silently replayed it over and over inside their minds.

90. The accolade for 'longest TV series title ever' belongs to America's *Hey Michael – When Ya Gonna Throw That Tramp Wife o' Yours in the Dumpster and Move Back Down to Wisconsin to Live With Your Silver-Haired Mom and Your Sister and Her Husband and Their Three Daughters Steffi, Sam, and Priscilla (Priscilla Being the One with Auburn Hair – Well, Not Really Auburn – I Guess You Could Say It's Kinda Mousy) and – Michael? Michael? Are You There? Whaddaya Mean I Got the Wrong Number? Hey! Woah! I'm Sorry! Jesus, I'm Such a Schmuck! No Hard Feelings, Huh, Buddy? The Next Generation*

91. In 1992, US soap *Preservation Hospital* made history by employing real doctors and nurses. A year later, rival soap *Ward 19* went one better by featuring real surgeons performing real operations. Both were beaten in the ratings by a new soap called *Cashchuck Clinic*, which fired real banknotes through the screen, directly onto viewers' carpets.

92. Research shows newborn babies often believe the figures on television represent transitory phantoms intent on distracting their parents from the important things in life.

93. A recent survey in a Northumbria school revealed not a single child could begin to imagine a world without TV – even after watching a programme showing what it might be like.

94. Japanese scientists have created a television that fits inside a contact lens. It cannot be switched off and issues the wearer with instructions that absolutely must be obeyed.

95. Sometimes, when watching TV, you can catch sight of your own reflection. That's fine, but the minute you start waving at it you've got problems.

96. Indonesian televisions come equipped with Venetian blinds that automatically close whenever a nude body appears on screen.

97. Ask a man from Nairobi to look up the football scores on Teletext and he'll immediately and without question, urinate on your left leg. That's because 'Teletext' is Swahili for 'urinate on my left leg'. And 'look up the football scores on' is Swahili for 'immediately and without question'.

98. US education channel The Thinkbox is broadcasting the world's first televised encyclopaedia, covering every conceivable subject imaginable. At time of going to press, the programme had been running for sixteen years and has just reached the word Bunion.

99. On spotting a television set in the window of a store in Brazil, it is considered good luck to break the neck of the next animal you pass.

100. Like many other US shows of its era, hit 60s sitcom *Saunder's Backyard* used 'canned laughter' to provide atmosphere. But behind the chuckles lurked a chilling secret – the laughs were provided cheaply by a Texan sound effects company that recorded inmates on death row laughing nihilistically at mocked-up drawings of themselves as old-age pensioners.

101. Crazy board game fanatics in the Dutch town of Urecht once used a large portable TV as a giant dice in a game of Monopoly. The game was abandoned when mum returned unexpectedly.

You're you.

Be who you are.

Thinking

Breathing

Being

Everyone's individua
and you're no exceptior

Despot™ create products that help you
express how much of yourself you are

Without us you're nothing

Remember tha

Despot

Pretending you're free

If you enjoyed this book, you might also enjoy the following:

KEEP BRITAIN DOGLESS: THE REAL TED BELLINGHAM
By Daralis Crouse
£6.99

The shocking and completely unauthorised biography of the Keep Britain Tidy superstar that kicked the dog-loving world off its pistons is now available in paperback. Daralis Crouse, Bellingham's former bodyguard, holds nothing back in this tell-all expose of the hound-hating truth behind the familiar squeaky-clean image.
Includes crude sketches of Ted Bellingham killing a poodle with a hockey stick and pissing on a can of Pedigree Chum.

YING-TONG'S GUIDE TO RIFE
By Ying Tong
£44.99

"Ahhh-so!" – *Maxim*
"Ahhh-so!" – *Scorch*
"Ahhh-so!" – *FHM*

Ahhhh-so! Fresh from his successful TVGH 4 comedy series, Dunstable's most hilarious wannabe Chinaman presents his very own guide to life, in the 26-page Christmas stocking-filler to end all 26-page Christmas stocking-fillers.
Contains 24 full-page colour photographs of Ying Tong wearing a big oriental hat and pulling comical "Chinese" faces, plus a spoof takeaway menu and a contents page.

SHAPES DESCRIBED
By Simeon Venn-Diagram
£12.99

"Spellbinding" – *The Observer*
"Mesmerising" – *The Independent*
"Hypnotic" – *Acorn-Pricked Pompous Book Ponce Quarterly*

Circles, triangles, squares.
Ovals.
Oh, and hexagons.
Shapes come in many guises. They are sometimes rounded; sometimes angular. But what, precisely, are they? In a fascinating collection of extended essays, Simeon Venn-Diagram attempts to describe every shape known to man using ostentatious words alone. His results uncover the essential truth at the heart of all shapes – that the shapes we see are as much forms witnessed by us as they are outlines viewed by our eyes.

THE FAT MAN WHAT DONE A GUFF
By Adam Timberland
£7.99

Eight-year-old Timberland's debut novel will have you in stitches as it recounts the tale of a fat man what done a big guff in a supermarket. The guff come out so hard it knocked a tin of peas off a shelf and it stinked so much it made an old lady go sick on the floor.
As heard on A Book at Bedtime.

WENDY WESTWOOD'S WILD WEDDING WALKABOUT
By Mimsy Infection
£7.99

"A hoot" – *Ms. Singleton Magazine*
"Hilarious" – *Female Loner*
"When it finishes, you'll go back and read it all over again because your real life is pointless by comparison" – *Hormonal Weeper*

Wendy Westwood thought she'd never get married. But that was in the days Before Dan. Now the big day's due in a fortnight's time and Wendy's got pre-wedding jitters. And when it all gets too much, Wendy goes AWOL – by running away to a remote Scottish island! How crazy is that? Answer: VERY!
A knockabout chase across the British Isles develops as Wendy's equally crazy friends struggle to ensure she makes it to the church on time! Whoops! Hee hee!
Contains a funny bit where Wendy snogs a male stripper – but he later turns out to be gay! And a poignant bit where Wendy's unapologetically promiscuous chain-smoking friend Robyn breaks down in tears and admits she wishes she was the one getting married. And another funny bit where all four girls hitch a lift from a truck driver by hoisting their skirts up over their thighs. And loads of other bits that are just too shitbone fucking awful to go into right now.

25,000 THINGS TO SHOUT AT A STRANGER'S CHILD THAT'S ANNOYING YOU IN A RESTAURANT BY RUNNING AROUND SHRIEKING ITS HEAD OFF
By Milo Garotte
£2.99

Includes "Shut it", "Sit down", "Be quiet", "Belt up", and many, many more.